Ukraine

Ukraine

BY PATRICIA K. KUMMER

Enchantment of the World
Second Series

Children's Press®
A Division of Scholastic Inc.

NEW YORK   TORONTO   LONDON   AUCKLAND   SYDNEY
MEXICO CITY   NEW DELHI   HONG KONG
DANBURY, CONNECTICUT

Frontispiece: Hand-painted Ukrainian Easter eggs

Consultant: Myroslava M. Mudrak, M.A. Columbia University, Ph.D. University of Texas at Austin

Please note: All statistics are as up-to-date as possible at the time of publication.

Visit Children's Press on the Internet: http://publishing.grolier.com

Book Production by Herman Adler Design

Library of Congress Cataloging-in-Publication Data

Kummer, Patricia K.
    Ukraine / by Patricia K. Kummer.
      p. cm. — (Enchantment of the world. Second series)
    Includes bibliographical references and index.
    ISBN 0-516-21101-3
    1. Ukraine—Juvenile literature. [1. Ukraine.] I. Title. II. Series.
DK508.12 .K86   2001
947.7—dc21

                                      00-057040

Acknowledgments

I wish to thank the many people in the United States, Canada, and Ukraine who helped me gain a clearer understanding of recent events and current trends in Ukraine, as well as a flavor of daily life and local customs—especially Lena Baranova, her son Artyom, and her many students in Kirovohrad; Maureen Barney, the first U.S. high school teacher selected to demonstrate U.S. teaching methods at the Kyiv Pedagogical Institute; Mykhaylo Klimchak, Katya Krenina, Annette Smilyakova, Irena Sonevytsky; and the volunteers and staff of the Ukrainian National Museum in Chicago. Special thanks go to my husband Walt, for his patience and support as I researched and wrote this book.

Cover photo:
Saint Andrew's
Church, Kyiv

Contents

CHAPTER

A view of Lviv

A gold Scythian vase

Reclaiming Ukraine's Identity

B LACK-ROBED PRIESTS LED THE PROCESSION INTO THE soccer stadium. They chanted and carried crosses and candles. Several rock bands and colorfully dressed folksingers followed the priests around the stadium's track. It was the opening-night ceremony for the 1991 Chervona Ruta Music Festival in Zaporizhzhya, Ukraine.

During that August evening, heavy metal bands and other rockers entertained the crowd. Their songs criticized life under Soviet rule. Folksingers in traditional costumes were accompanied by *banduras*—large stringed instruments. Their songs reminded the audience of Ukraine's strong cultural traditions. All songs—rock and folk—were sung in Ukrainian. Between songs, the priests prayed and spoke about the need to revive Ukrainian culture. At various times during the evening, men dressed as *Kozaks* (Cossacks) rode horses around the track. They dismounted and remounted while their horses moved at great speeds, just as the

Opposite: **A Ukrainian musician playing a bandura**

A modern-day Kozak attempts to pick up a hat while riding.

Kozaks might have done in battle. The Kozaks were warriors who fought for Ukraine against Poland, Russia, and the Tatars from the 1500s through the 1700s. Zaporizhzhya was then the center of Kozak culture.

The music festival had two purposes. One purpose was to inspire pride in Ukrainian culture and history. The other was to show how Soviet rule had tried to bury the feeling of being Ukrainian. Until 1989, Russian was the official language of the Soviet Union, which included Ukraine. The Russian Orthodox Church was the only religion allowed in the Soviet Union. Not until 1989 and 1990 were the Ukrainian Catholic and Ukrainian Autocephalous Orthodox Churches again allowed to function in Ukraine.

Chervona Ruta successfully met both purposes. Throughout the opening night, the audience became bolder. Many shouted, "Ukraine without Moscow!" Some waved the blue-and-yellow flag of Ukraine, which had been banned under Soviet rule. Police officers who stood along the sidelines did nothing to stop these displays. Some members of the audience felt uncomfortable, however. Many of them had been brought up to speak Russian, and they feared what might happen if Ukraine broke with the Soviet Union.

People rally in support of a new Ukrainian constitution.

Ukraine

LATVIA

LITHUANIA

BELARUS

POLAND

RUSSIA

Prypyat

Prypyal Marshes

Lutsk

Chronobyl

Chernihiv

Psel

Sumy

Rivne

Kyiv (Kiev)

Ternopil

Lviv

Zhytomyr

Poltava

Kharkiv

Khmelnytsky

SLOVAKIA

Dnister

Vinnitsa

Cherkasy

Dnipro

Donets

Luhansk

Kamyanets-Podilsky

Kirovograd

Yaremcha

Uman

Dneprodzerzhinsk

Makeyevka

Gorlovka

HUNGARY

Chernivtsi

Southern Buh

Dnipropetrovsk

Donetsk

Rakhiv

Nicopol

Kryvyy Rih

Zaporizhzhya

MOLDAVA

Mykolayiv

Mariupol

ROMANIA

Prut

Kherson

Sea of Azov

Odesa

Krymian Peninsula

Danube

Yevpatoria

Simferopol

Kerch

Sevastopol

Feodosiya

Alushta

BULGARIA

Alupka

Yalta

BLACK SEA

N

W   E

S

UKRAINE

- Cities of over 500,000 people
- Smaller cities and towns

0   100 miles

0   150 kilometers

TURKEY

At that time, Ukraine was a republic in the Soviet Union. On August 19, 1991—the day after Chervona Ruta ended—some members of the Soviet government in Moscow attempted a coup. By August 22, this attempt to seize the government had failed. The coup attempt, however, showed the weakness of the Soviet government and of Communism. Two days later, on August 24, the Ukrainian legislature voted for independence from the Soviet Union. Ukraine became an independent country. Even the people who had shouted, "Ukraine without Moscow!" a few days earlier, were surprised at this sudden turn of events. They thought the move to Ukrainian independence would take at least a few years.

New and in the Middle

Ukraine is one of the world's newest nations, having proclaimed its independence in 1991. Yet Ukraine's history is thousands of years old. Throughout most of that time, however, it was not a free country. Foreign powers controlled Ukraine and the Ukrainian people. But the people of Ukraine always held onto their cultural heritage. They spoke Ukrainian whenever they could. They practiced folk arts for which they are still famous, such as brightly patterned Easter eggs and intricate embroidery. Many Ukrainians even secretly practiced their religion.

Because Ukraine lies between Poland and Russia, it is often called an eastern European country. Actually, Ukraine lies in the middle of Europe. In fact, Europe's geographical

A village in the Carpathian Mountains

center is in Ukraine's Carpathian Mountains near the town of Rakhiv. Ukraine's central geographical position in Europe is important. Many political scientists in western Europe and the United States believe that a strong, independent Ukraine is the key to peace in this part of the world. Since its independence, Ukraine has developed closer ties with western Europe. The new country already has a strong relationship with the North Atlantic Treaty Organization (NATO) and with the European Union (EU). Of course, Ukraine still has strong ties with Russia, too. About 22 percent of Ukraine's population is Russian, and Russia remains a large trading partner with Ukraine.

There Is No "The" in Ukraine

For hundreds of years, Ukraine was called "The Ukraine." This name referred to the land that now makes up the country of Ukraine. After claiming its independence, "The" was officially dropped as part of the country's name. By doing that, Ukraine's government let the world's nations know that Ukraine was now not just an area of land but an independent nation.

Since its independence, other place names in Ukraine have also been changed. On maps of Ukraine, names of towns, cities, rivers, and other geographic forms now have Ukrainian spellings—not Russian spellings. For example, the Ukrainian spelling for Ukraine's capital is Kyiv. For centuries, that city's name had been spelled in Russian—Kiev. Street signs and markers for parks and monuments are also now spelled in Ukrainian rather than Russian.

Ancient Symbols for a New Nation

Now that Ukraine is an independent nation, the government and people are reviving Ukraine's traditions. One of these traditions is the symbol of the *tryzub*, or trident—a three-pronged spear. According to Ukraine's Constitution, the national emblem is a gold trident on a blue background. This symbol has been used in Ukraine since the first century A.D. Later, princes of Ukraine sealed important papers with the trident symbol. They also stamped the trident on coins. Kozaks used the trident on their flags and coats of arms. During the brief years of the Ukrainian National Republic (1918–1921), the trident appeared on that government's money. Because the trident was a symbol of Ukrainian national pride, Russian tsars and then the Soviet government outlawed the symbol.

Ukraine's new currency, the *hryvnia*, also has a long tradition. *Hryvnia* was the name for coins issued by Prince Volodymyr the Great. Volodymyr had his coins stamped with the trident symbol. Today, the trident appears on the back of Ukraine's coins, called *kopiykas*.

By reviving rich traditions from their past, the Ukrainian people are reclaiming their language, religion, history, and culture. They hope to use the past to build a strong, united nation for the future.

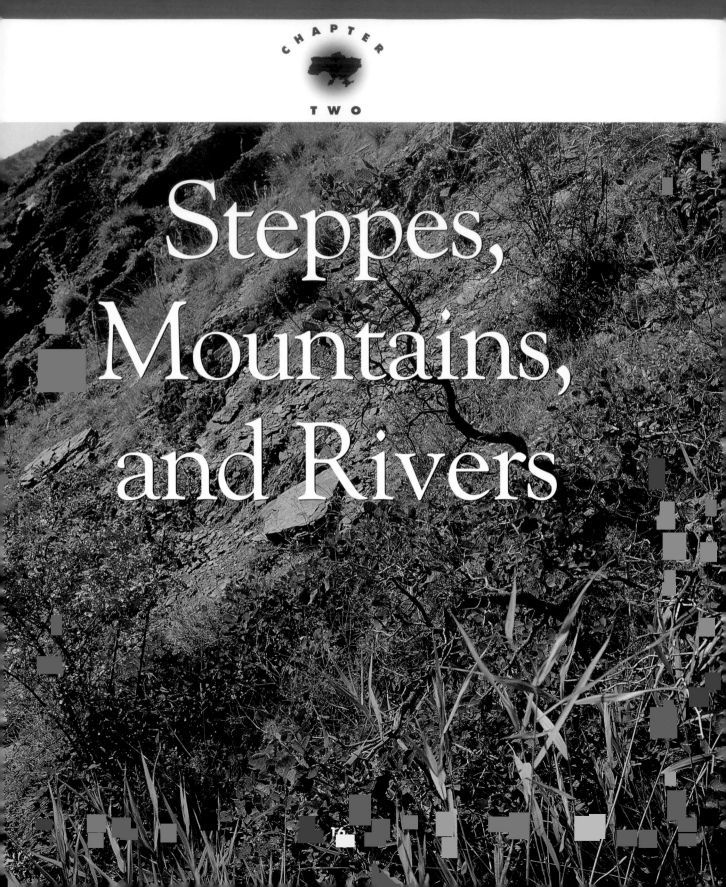

Steppes, Mountains, and Rivers

UKRAINE COVERS 233,090 SQUARE MILES (603,656 square kilometers) of the southeastern portion of the Eastern European Plain. This makes Ukraine the largest European country, slightly larger than France. Although Russia is much larger than Ukraine, most of Russia lies in Asia, not Europe. Texas, in the United States, and the Canadian province of Manitoba, are a bit larger than Ukraine.

Within Ukraine are six topographic areas that stretch mainly east–west across the country. They range from lowlands along the rivers and seas to low mountain peaks. About two-thirds of Ukraine, however, is covered with flat, fertile plains and plateaus. This part of Ukraine is called the *steppe*. Ukraine's steppe is much like the Great Plains of North America—grassland with few trees. The steppe runs northeast to southwest. Its northern edge reaches from just north of Kharkiv to where the Dnister River enters Moldava. All land south to the Black Sea and the Sea of Azov is considered steppe.

Throughout history, Ukraine's land has not provided protection from invaders. Because there are no high mountain ranges or rough, defensible land, outsiders have conquered Ukraine many times. In fact, Ukraine's name comes from the ancient Slavic word *okraina*, which means "borderland." From early times, the people of Ukraine have viewed their land as one caught between powerful neighbors.

Ukraine's Borders

Today, Ukraine's borders are secure. Neighboring countries have neither time nor desire to invade Ukraine. They are trying to build stable democratic governments and to reform their economies, just as Ukraine is doing. Ukraine's longest border, 979 miles (1,576 km), is with Russia to the east and northeast. Russia was the leading republic in the former Union of Soviet Socialist Republics (USSR). Belarus, to the north of Ukraine, and Moldava, to the southwest, were also republics in the former USSR. Romania is another southwestern neighbor. Poland, Slovakia, and Hungary lie to the west. All four of these countries ousted Communist governments in the late 1980s and early 1990s. Many ethnic Ukrainians still live in these newly free countries.

Waterways also form Ukraine's borders. The Prut and Danube Rivers each separate Ukraine from Romania for brief stretches. The waters of the Black Sea and the Sea of Azov form Ukraine's

A Ukrainian vessel on the Danube

southern border. Together, the two seas give Ukraine a coastline of 1,729 miles (2,782 km). To the southeast, the Kerch Strait divides Ukraine's Kerch Peninsula from Russia. The Kerch Strait also connects the Black Sea to the Sea of Azov.

Upland and Lowland

The Northern Ukrainian Upland covers northeastern Ukraine. This upland is a low plateau with land that is good for

Ukraine's Geographical Features

Area: 233,090 square miles (603,656 sq km) within Europe

Longest Border: 979 miles (1,576 km), with Russia

Greatest Distance North to South: 550 miles (885 km)

Greatest Distance East to West: 830 miles (1,336 km)

Coastline: 1,729 miles (2,782 km)

Largest Lake: Lake Sasik, 79 square miles (205 sq km)

Heaviest Precipitation: 59 inches (150 centimeters) each year in the Carpathian Mountains

growing grains and sugar beets. Important natural gas deposits lie below the plateau. Kharkiv, the country's second-largest city, is in this part of Ukraine. Other important northern upland cities include Poltava and Sumy.

Northwestern Ukraine is known as the Dnipro-Prypyat Lowland. This geographic area lies between the Dnipro and the Prypyat Rivers. It was once heavily forested, but trees now cover only about 25 percent of the lowland. Most of these trees are in Ukraine's part

A hay field in the Poltava region

of the Prypyat Marshes, which cover far northwestern Ukraine. This marshland also extends into Belarus. The Prypyat Marshes are the largest area of marshland in Europe. Some of the marshland has been drained, and farmers use this reclaimed land as grazing land for their cattle. Kyiv, Ukraine's capital, stands on the Dnipro River in the northwestern lowland. Chernihiv, Cherkasy, and Zhytomyr are other major lowland cities. A large part of the Dnipro-Prypyat Lowland was contaminated with radioactive material when the nuclear reactor at Chornobyl exploded.

The Central Plateau

South of the Dnipro-Prypyat Lowland and the Northern Ukrainian Upland lies the Central Plateau. This is Ukraine's largest topographic region. Most of Ukraine's steppe is in this area. The Central Plateau stretches from Ukraine's border with Russia in the east to its border with Poland in the west. Included in the Central Plateau are areas of highland known as the Azov Upland, the Dnipro Upland, and the Volyn-Podilsk Upland. Rivers have cut deep gorges and ravines through the highlands.

The Central Plateau also contains most of Ukraine's richest natural resources. A wide band of *chornozem*, or black soil, covers the eastern Central Plateau. This thick, deep,

A field of sunflowers

The World's Worst Nuclear Accident

At 1:23 A.M. on Saturday, April 26, 1986, Reactor Number 4 at the Chornobyl nuclear power plant exploded. The reactor's heavy steel and concrete lid blew off. About 10 tons (9 metric tons) of radioactive material shot upward—ten times the amount of radioactive material released in the U.S. bombing of Hiroshima and Nagasaki during World War II. Winds carried radioactive fallout to nearby Belarus, Russia, and Poland and as far as France, Italy, and the northern Baltic countries. Fallout from the explosion and fire contaminated about 100,000 square miles (258,980 sq km) of land. About 18,647 square miles (48,292 sq km) of that land is in Ukraine. Animals, crops, and other plants were also contaminated.

The Chornobyl plant is near the town of Prypyat, which is only 10 miles (16 km) northwest of the city of Chornobyl and 65 miles (105 km) north of Kyiv. The explosion put millions of Ukrainians at risk. The day after the explosion, the Soviet government began to evacuate Prypyat. In all, 135,000 people were moved from the immediate area. They could take nothing with them because everything was contaminated. Today, Prypyat is a ghost town.

Thirty-one people died immediately from the explosion, fire, and radiation poisoning. They were plant workers, firefighters, and first-aid workers. Those people did not know they were being exposed to radiation and did not wear the proper protective equipment. Later, the Soviet government sent over 650,000 people, mainly young soldiers, to clean up the contamination at the plant. Once again, they were not provided proper clothing. Since 1986, more than 12,500 of these men have died from radiation poisoning. Thousands of children and adults in the area also became contaminated. Many later developed leukemia and thyroid cancer and died.

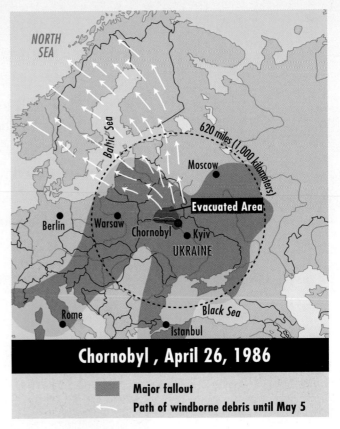

Chornobyl , April 26, 1986

- Major fallout
- Path of windborne debris until May 5

black soil is the world's most fertile land. Large crops of wheat, corn, barley, rye, and sunflowers grow on the rich chornozem. More treasures lie under the Central Plateau. Large coal deposits are mined in the Donets Basin, which is close to the Russian border. Iron mining takes place near Kryvyy Rih. The Central Plateau is one of Ukraine's most populated areas. Major cities in the eastern part of the area include Luhansk, Donetsk, Zaporizhzhya, and Kryvyy Rih. Large cities in the western part of the Central Plateau include Lviv, Lutsk, Ternopil, Khmelnytsky, and Kamyanets-Podilsky.

The Coastal Plain

The Coastal Plain is south of the Central Plateau. All lands along the Black Sea and the Sea of Azov make up the Coastal Plain. This includes the northern two-thirds of the Krymian (also known as Crimea) Peninsula. Ukraine's lowest point is sea level, along the Black Sea.

The rest of Ukraine's steppe is on the Coastal Plain. Because this part of Ukraine receives little rainfall, it is called *desert steppe*. Many farms on the Coastal Plain rely on water from irrigation canals. Several cities on the Coastal Plain are

A shrimp market in Odesa

important shipping centers. Odesa is the largest of these, and others are Mykolayiv, Kherson, and Mariupol, as well as Kerch, on the Krymian Peninsula. All five cities have large ports.

Mountains

About 8 percent of Ukraine is covered with mountains. They are in two groups—the Carpathian Mountains and the Krymian Mountains. The Carpathians rise over southwestern Ukraine and extend into Poland, Slovakia, and Romania. Mount Hoverlya in the Carpathians, is Ukraine's highest point, rising 6,762 feet (2,061 meters) above sea level. Small-scale farming, including vineyards, takes place in the mountain valleys. Most farmers make their living herding sheep and cattle. Logging continues to be an important industry in the Carpathians; but overcutting of trees has caused mudslides and flooding. Hotels and resorts with health-giving mineral springs dot the area. Uzhhorod, at the foot of the mountains, attracts visitors from nearby Slovakia and Hungary. Hikers and campers enjoy the fresh air and clean rivers near the mountain town of Yaremcha.

The Krymian Mountains stand along the southern shore of the Krymian Peninsula. Their highest peak is Mount Roman-Kosh. It rises 5,069 feet (1,545 m) above sea level. Vineyards and apple and cherry orchards grow on the hillsides. Between the mountains and the Black Sea lie narrow beaches. Important cities along these coastal mountains include Feodosiya, Alushta, Yalta, and Alupka. Tourism is the main industry that supports this southernmost part of Ukraine.

More than 20,000 rivers and streams flow through Ukraine. The country's four major rivers, from west to east, are the Dnister, the Southern Buh, the Dnipro, and the Donets. All four rivers flow from north to south into the Black Sea or the Sea of Azov. A few rivers in western Ukraine flow north and eventually empty into the Baltic Sea. The Danube River, in far southwestern Ukraine, also empties into the Black Sea.

The Dnipro is Ukraine's longest river and Europe's third longest river. Only the Volga and Danube Rivers are longer. The Dnipro flows for 609 miles (980 km) through Ukraine, dividing the country unevenly into east and west. Half of Ukraine's other rivers drain into the Dnipro. Since ancient times, the Dnipro has been an important trade route. Today, shipping and trade remain important in the Dnipro port cities of Kyiv, Dnipropetrovsk, Zaporizhzhya, and Kherson. Boats called *hydrofoils* carry passengers between Kyiv and Cherkasy. Other boats take passengers as far as Kherson on the Dnipro.

The Dnister River begins in Ukraine's Carpathian Mountains. It winds its way through southwestern Ukraine before entering Moldava. From there, the Dnister flows back into Ukraine and empties into the Black Sea southwest of Odesa. Much shipping takes place on the Dnister. The Southern Buh also starts in southwestern Ukraine. It travels 532 miles (856 km) completely within Ukraine and empties into the Black Sea at Mykolayiv. Many rapids on the upper Southern Buh make shipping impossible there. However, those waters have been harnessed to produce hydroelectric power. The Donets is the major river in eastern Ukraine. It begins in Russia, twists through the Donets Basin of eastern Ukraine, and then reenters Russia before emptying into the Sea of Azov. The Donets is an important transportation route among the industrial cities of eastern Ukraine. Ships and barges on the Donets carry coal, iron ore, and heavy manufactured products.

Ukraine has about 3,000 small natural lakes. The country's largest lakes lie near the delta of the Danube River. Both freshwater and saltwater lakes have formed in the delta. Lake Sasik is Ukraine's largest saltwater lake, covering 79 square miles (205 sq km). The largest freshwater lake is Yalpuh at 58 square miles (150 sq km). Lake Brebeneskul, the country's highest lake, is found in the Carpathian Mountains. Lake Sityaz, in far northwestern Ukraine, is the country's deepest lake.

Launching a new ship from a Mykolayiv shipyard

Ukraine also has several large reservoirs. These are lakes formed behind dams on rivers. Some of the largest reservoirs are on the Dnipro. They include the Kremenchuk, Kakhovka, Kyiv, Kaniv, Dniprodzerzhynsk, and Dnipro Reservoirs. The Dnister Reservoir is on the Dnister River. Ukraine uses water from reservoirs to irrigate farm fields, to produce hydroelectric power, and to provide drinking water.

A bird soars above the strong current of the Danube.

Northern and western Ukraine have cold winters and cool to warm summers. Precipitation falls year round, but most of it comes as rain in summer. Most of Ukraine receives from 16 to 24 inches (41 to 61 centimeters) of rain and snow a year. Northwestern Ukraine receives the heaviest summer rainfall, with a yearly average of 24 inches (61 cm). The Carpathian Mountains receive the most rain and snow, with a yearly average of about 59 inches (150 cm).

Ukraine's southern and eastern steppes receive little rain—less than 12 inches (30 cm) each year. Farmers there rely on irrigation to water their crops. In addition, *sukhoviyi*—or hot, dry winds—blow from the east across the steppes. These winds often damage crops and lead to drought conditions.

The southern coast of the Krymian Peninsula, however, has a climate similar to that of Italy, Greece, and Turkey. Ukrainians on the Krymian Peninsula enjoy hot, dry summers and mild, rainy winters. Little snow falls that far south. The peninsula's climate has made it a popular vacation spot since the 1860s.

Looking at Ukraine's Cities

Kharkiv, Ukraine's second-largest city, is located in eastern Ukraine only 25 miles (40 km) from the Russian border. Founded in 1656 by a Kozak, Kharkiv quickly came under Russian influence and remained loyal to the tsars through the 1700s. Between 1921 and 1934, Kharkiv served as the capital of the Ukrainian Soviet Socialist Republic. Since World War II, Kharkiv has been a center for the production of heavy metal products. Farm machinery, locomotives, and machine tools are a few important products. Kharkiv is sometimes called the "Boston" of Ukraine because it has many institutions of higher learning. They include Kharkiv University, which was founded in 1805. Kharkiv also has many beautiful churches. They include the red-and-cream striped Blahovishchenskyy Cathedral and Uspensky Cathedral, which has a 292-feet- (89-meter-) tall bell tower.

Dnipropetrovsk, about 120 miles (193 km) southwest of Kharkiv, is Ukraine's third-largest city. It sits on the big bend of the Dnipro River. From its founding in 1787 until 1926, the city was named Ekaterinoslav for Catherine the Great, Empress of Russia. Today, Dnipropetrovsk is Ukraine's largest industrial city. Railroads link the city to nearby iron and coal mines and rich wheat fields. Products made in the city include: chemicals, food products, steel, and heavy machinery.

Odesa (below), often called the Pearl of the Black Sea, is in southwestern Ukraine. It is Ukraine's fifth-largest city. The city started as a Tatar fort in the 1300s.

It received its name in 1795, after the Russian Empire gained control of this part of Ukraine. Always a busy seaport and fishing center, Odesa became industrialized while under Soviet control. Today, Odesa is also an important tourist center. Its warm summer weather and beautiful beaches attract many vacationers. Odesa is one of Ukraine's most ethnically diverse cities, with Ukrainians, Russians, Bulgarians, Moldovans, and Jews making up the largest population groups.

Lviv (above) is the largest city in western Ukraine. It is about 53 miles (85 km) from Poland. Founded in 1256 by Prince Danylo of Galicia-Volhynia, Lviv is one of Ukraine's oldest and most historic cities. Danylo named the city for his son Lev. Throughout history, Lviv came under Polish, Austrian, German, and Soviet rule. During the many centuries of foreign control, Lviv remained the center of Ukrainian culture. In 1596, it became the seat of the Ukrainian Catholic Church. During the late nineteenth and early twentieth centuries, Lviv became a center for the Ukrainian nationalist movement. In the 1980s, groups in Lviv played important parts in winning Ukrainian independence. Today, Lviv retains many aspects of a European city from the Middle Ages or Renaissance, with narrow, winding streets, castles, and churches

Steppes, Mountains, and Rivers **27**

The Natural Environment

BECAUSE UKRAINE HAS LOW MOUNTAINS AND IS MAINLY open steppe, winds have carried plant seeds to and from Ukraine's neighboring countries. Animals have freely migrated to and from these same places. Today, Ukraine has about 16,000 kinds of plants and about 28,000 kinds of animals. They live and grow in Ukraine's forests, steppes, mountains, and rivers and streams.

Life in the Forests

Only 14 percent of Ukraine is covered with forests. Most of this woodland is in northern and western Ukraine. These forests have the country's greatest variety of trees. Many kinds of beech, oak, birch, maple, linden, elm, aspen, pine, spruce,

A Ukrainian forest

Opposite: **A marmot emerges from its underground home.**

A Symbol of the Nation

The *kalyna*, or guelder rose, is a flowering bush. In the spring, the kalyna is covered with white flowers. By summer, the flowers have become clusters of shiny, red berries that last throughout the winter. Ukrainian poets have compared the berries' staying power to the strength of the Ukrainian people and nation. Throughout the centuries, the kalyna has become an unofficial symbol of Ukraine.

Storks

Storks, or *leleky* in Ukrainian, are found throughout Ukraine. They build huge nests high in trees, atop telephone poles, or on rooftops near the chimney. Each spring the stork returns to the same nest. In Ukrainian folklore, the stork symbolizes life and hope for the future. Maybe that's why Ukrainians say that when a stork returns to its nest atop a home, a baby will be born.

and fir grow in these forests. In parts of the forests, yellow rhododendron bloom and blackberries and huckleberries ripen. Some of the northwestern forest grows in swamps or on marshland, such as the Prypyat Marshes. Cattails, cotton grass, and reed grass thrive in these wetlands.

Deer feeding in the woodlands of Ukraine

Bear, elk, and lynx live deep in the western forest. Deer, foxes, wild boars, and wolves are more commonly seen. Beavers, mink, and otters make homes near the lakes and rivers. Bald coots, black storks, and wild ducks nest near these waterways. Eels and Baltic sturgeons swim in western rivers that flow north toward the Baltic Sea.

Mountain Plants and Animals

The rest of Ukraine's forests are in the Carpathian and Krymian Mountains. Oak and beech trees grow at the lowest elevations. Higher up are fir, sycamore, spruce, and dwarf pines. Mediterrean types of pines and junipers also grow in the Krymian Mountains. Acacia, cypress, and magnolia trees hug the Krymian's southern slopes. Meadows of flowers and grasses carpet the ground between these mountains' forests. In the spring, gentians, saffron, and thistles bloom in Carpathian meadows. At high elevations in the Carpathians, edelweiss grows. Ukrainians call this delicate white bloom the magic silk flower. In the Big Krymian Canyon, ferns and orchids flourish.

Edelweiss bloom in the Carpathian landscape.

Golden eagles, short-toed eagles, and booted eagles soar above the Carpathians. White-backed and red-capped woodpeckers thrive among the forests. Grey wagtails and kingfishers are found near mountain streams. Brown bears live deep in the Carpathian's forests. Roe deer, red deer, and wild boar feed in forests at lower elevations. Trout, grayling, and Danube salmon swim in the Carpathian's rivers and streams. Krymian red and roe deer and Krymian

A short-toed eagle feeding its young

A tawny owl grasps an evergreen branch.

mountain foxes are the largest animals in the Krymian Mountains. Griffon vultures, tawny owls, and Krymian jays are a few birds found in these mountains.

Plants and Animals of the Steppe

Many kinds of drought-resistant grasses, such as fescue and feather grasses, grow on the steppe. Flowers such as alyssum, crocuses, forget-me-nots, irises, hyacinths, poppies, sunflowers, and tulips burst forth in brilliant color in the spring. Oak, elm, black poplar, alder, and willow trees grow in clumps near the steppe's rivers.

Birds of the steppe include the demoiselle crane and little bustard. The steppe's main songbird is the lark. Steppe eagles

Ukraine's Famous Oak Tree

The towering Zaporizhzhya Oak stands on the west side of the Dnipro River near the Dniprohes Dam outside Zaporizhzhya. This oak tree is 600 to 700 years old, measures 21 feet (6.4 m) around, and is 118 feet (36 m) tall. The Zaporizhzhya Oak plays an important part in Kozak legends. Some stories have seventeenth-century war hero Bohdan Khmelnytsky rallying his troops under the tree before their battle with the Poles in 1648.

swoop down to snatch up their next meal, usually ground squirrels called *sousliks*. Besides sousliks, other steppe mammals include marmots and hamsters. They eat the seeds, stems, leaves, and bulbs of steppe plants and grasses. The Bobak marmot looks like an American prairie dog. Marmots dig deep tunnels underground, where they live in colonies. They warn one another of danger with a loud piercing cry. This sound can be heard for one-third of a mile (0.53 km).

National Parks and Nature Reserves

National parks and nature reserves cover about 3 million acres (1.2 million hectares), or about 2 percent, of Ukraine's land. They are located along Ukraine's seacoasts and in its forests, steppes, and mountains. Since its independence, Ukraine's

The Novy Svet Nature Preserve

government has passed more laws to preserve and expand these reserves and parks. The main purpose of the reserves and parks is to protect plants and animals. The national parks are open to tourists and offer resorts and activities for rest and recreation.

The oldest and the newest national parks are in the Carpathian Mountains. Carpathian National Park is located in the southeastern part of the mountains. Founded in 1980, it is the oldest and the largest of Ukraine's national parks. The Carpathian's highest peaks are in this park. Skolivsk Beskidy National Park was established in 1999. It's in the northwestern Carpathians and connects with national parks across the border in Poland and Slovakia.

On the border with Belarus, the Polissya Nature Reserve protects marshy forests and the animals that live there. Along the Black Sea lie two nature reserves created to protect many kinds of birds. Black-crowned night herons, squacco herons, and glossy ibis feed on frogs, fish, and insects in the Danube Water Meadows Nature Reserve. Sandwich terns, slender-billed gulls, mallards, and mute swans nest and breed in the Black Sea Nature Preserve. Other reserves protect steppe plants. More than 5,000 different kinds of plants grow in the Kaniv Nature Reserve. The Ukrainian Steppe Reserve covers three kinds of steppe near the northern shore of the Sea of Azov.

National Parks and Nature Reserves

Ukraine's Oldest Nature Reserve

The Falz-Fein Askania-Nova Biosphere Reserve is in southern Ukraine, just north of Krym. Askania-Nova started as a private reserve in 1874, when Friedrich von Falz-Fein, the landowner, set up a zoo. In 1887, a botanical garden was added to the reserve. The Ukrainian government named the area a national park in 1919 and renamed it as a reserve in 1921. In 1984, Askania-Nova became a United Nations biosphere reserve. Today, Askania-Nova covers 82,302 acres (33,308 ha) and includes a vast area of steppe that has never been plowed for crops. Amidst the steppe's grasses stand ancient stone monuments, called *kamianas babas* (old stone women, or stone grandmothers). Historians believe Scythians set up the stones to guard the steppe. Trees on the reserve include azalea, acacia, birch, and pine. An important program of the biosphere reserve is breeding rare and endangered species, such as the Przewalski's horse, the great bustard bird, and the Asian wild ass.

Sofiyyivka National Park is home to lovely lakes and lush trees.

Ukraine's cities also have large parks and botanical gardens. Many of them are part of the national park and nature reserve system. Sofiyyivka Arboretum and National Park is in the city of Uman. A Polish count built the park in 1796 as a sign of love for his wife, Sofiya. The park has about 500 kinds of trees, fountains, waterfalls, and lakes with islands. In Kyiv, 3 miles (5 km) of wooded parkland line the west bank of the Dnipro River. Wooded islands are found near the river's east bank. Chestnut trees line major streets in Ukraine's cities. In fact, the chestnut tree is the official symbol of Kyiv. Nikitsky Botanical Garden is near Yalta on the Krymian Peninsula. It is Ukraine's largest botanical garden. About 28,000 kinds of plants grow there, including 2,000 types of roses and a thousand-year-old pistachio tree.

Environmental Challenges

For seventy years, the Soviet Union exploited Ukraine's land, forests, and mineral resources. Thousands of factories polluted Ukraine's air and water with smoke and poisonous chemicals. The explosion at the Chornobyl nuclear power plant in 1986 contaminated much of northern and western Ukraine with radioactive waste. The Soviet Union's disregard for Ukraine's environment helped start the movement for independence in the 1980s.

In the late 1990s, Ukraine continued to have environmental problems. Air and water pollution led the list. Factories and mines in and near industrial cities—such as Zaporizhzhya and Kryvyy Rih and cities in the Donets Basin—still polluted the air, causing breathing problems for many Ukrainians. Ukraine also lacked an adequate supply of drinking water, especially in the cities. Fertilizers from farmland and waste from factories had seeped into many of Ukraine's rivers. The rivers deposited these wastes into the Black Sea and Sea of Azov. Overcutting of forests in northern and western Ukraine was another problem, leading to flooding and landslides during heavy rains. In 1998, Ukraine's worst natural disaster occurred when floods and landslides destroyed buildings, dams, and bridges in the west. Roads and railways were washed away. Thousands of people had to leave their homes.

Since its independence, Ukraine's government has passed laws to protect the environment. It has also set up fines to punish people who disobey the laws. However, bad economic times have left the government with little money to enforce environmental laws.

Smoking chimneys pollute the city of Zaporizhzhya's air.

Emergency workers dig for victims of a landslide that occurred in December, 1998.

Crossroads
of History

SINCE ANCIENT TIMES, UKRAINE HAS BEEN A CROSS-roads between Asia and Europe and between the Baltic Sea and the Black Sea. Traders from the north followed Ukraine's rivers and set up posts along them. Other traders built cities along the Black Sea. The vast open steppe allowed migrating people and warriors to easily enter what is now Ukraine. Throughout most of its history, Ukraine has been ruled by foreign powers.

Ukraine's Early People

People have lived in Ukraine for about 150,000 years. The best known of the early people were the Trypillians. Their name comes from the village of Trypillia, near Kyiv, where archaeologists found remains of their civilization. Historians think that the Trypillians were Europe's first farmers. Between about 5000 B.C. and 2000 B.C., they farmed and built villages on the steppe between the Dnister and the Dnipro Rivers. The Trypillians used wooden plows in their farm fields. They also made pottery decorated with black, white, and ocher designs. By 2000, the Trypillians had been overtaken by nomadic herders from the east.

Between about 1500 B.C. and A.D. 375, several groups of people pushed into Ukraine. The Cimmerians moved west across Ukraine. They controlled the steppe from the Dnister to Ukraine's present eastern border. The Cimmerians were the first to ride on horses in Ukraine and the first to use iron there.

A woman walks with her dog past a Scythian burial mound.

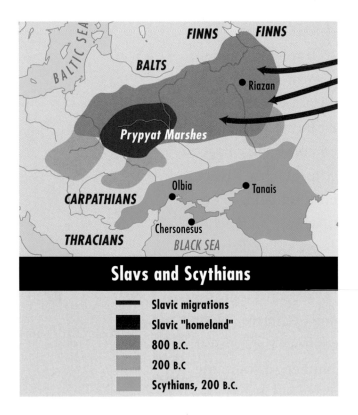

Slavs and Scythians

— Slavic migrations
■ Slavic "homeland"
▨ 800 B.C.
▨ 200 B.C
▨ Scythians, 200 B.C.

About 700 B.C., Scythian horsemen from the east gained control of the steppe. At the same time, Greek traders set up colonies along the Black Sea. Their main cities were near present-day Odesa, Mykolayiv, Chersonesus, Kerch, and Feodosiya. The Scythians forced tribute from the Cimmerians and other steppe people. Tribute was a kind of tax paid in furs, grain, wax, honey, and slaves. The Scythians then traded those goods with the Greeks for wine, gold, and silver. Today, Scythian burial mounds remain on the steppe. Some of them have been opened to reveal intricately formed gold statues.

Next came the Sarmatian horsemen. They ruled the steppe from about 200 B.C. to A.D. 200. The

Sarmatians wore long, loose trousers, leather vests, and leather boots and caps. By A.D 270, Goths from the Baltic Sea region had swept south through Ukraine to the Black Sea. About a hundred years later, the Huns invaded Ukraine from the east. They were followed in hundred-year intervals by the Bulgars and Avars.

The Slavic People

While the steppe was being continually invaded, a group of people was growing and developing in Ukraine's western forests. These people were Slavs. They lived between the Carpathian Mountains and the Prypyat Marshes. By the seventh century A.D., the Slavs had moved east, west, and south of those original lands. East Slavs eventually settled in what are now Ukraine, Russia, and Belarus. West Slavs today are known as Poles, Czechs, and Slovaks. South Slavs settled in what became Bulgaria, Macedonia, Serbia, and Croatia. The three groups of Slavs each developed its own language.

The East Slavs moved farther east into what became Ukraine. They were farmers and herders who also wove cloth and made pottery. They worshiped gods of nature, such as thunder and the sun. The East Slavs built log homes in small villages. At a central location between many villages, they erected stockades. The stockades provided protection from enemies and were meeting places to worship their gods. They later became centers of trade and political power. The city of Kyiv developed from one of those stockades.

The Legendary Founding of Kyiv

Early historians recorded that three East Slavic princes—Kyy, Shchek, and Khoriv—and their sister Lybid founded Kyiv at the end of the fifth century A.D. Kyy built a fortress on a hill that was called Kyiv.

Today, two other hills in Kyiv are named for Shchek and Khoriv. A small river that once flowed through Kyiv was named for Lybid. Today, a huge statue near the Dnipro River in Kyiv shows the city's founders standing in a boat.

Kyivan Rus

In the middle of the ninth century A.D., Varangian traders came from the Baltic region of present-day Sweden. They arrived in Ukraine in long rowboats. According to some historians, these traders were called "Rus." The name *Rus* came from an ancient Swedish word that meant "to row." The Rus of Kyiv already had trading centers in what is now northern Russia. They also traded with the Muslim Khazar Empire to the southeast of Ukraine. The Rus used the Dnipro River as a trade route to the Black Sea.

About 882, a decisive and gifted leader named Oleh took control of Kyiv and became the first Kyivan prince. By this time, the Kyivan Rus had absorbed the Slav tribes living around Kyiv. The Rus adopted the Slavic culture. They spoke the Slavic language and worshiped the same gods of nature. In 911, Oleh's army sailed to Constantinople (now Istanbul) and attacked the capital of the Byzantine Empire. Oleh forced Constantinople into a trade treaty that favored Kyiv. The following year, Oleh died.

Ihor, the next prince of Kyivan Rus, was a less successful ruler. The Byzantines burned the Kyivan fleet and forced Ihor to sign a trade treaty that favored them. At home, the Slavs refused to pay his unfair demands of tribute and finally killed him in 945. Olha, Ihor's wife, ruled Kyivan Rus strongly and wisely until 962. She reformed the system of tribute so that it was collected fairly. In 957, she traveled to Constantinople to work out terms for peace and trade. While she was there, Olha converted to Byzantine Christianity. Today, this religion is known as Eastern, or Greek, Orthodoxy. In 962, Svyatoslav, Ihor and Olha's son, became the ruler of Kyivan Rus. He brought all the East Slavs, to the northeast, under Kyivan rule. With his death in 972, a power

Kyivan Rus, 900–1054

- Kyivan Russia, 900
- added by 970 and later lost
- added by 1054

The Queen Olha monument in Kyiv

Volodymyr the Great

struggle erupted among Svyatoslav's three sons. In the end, Volodymyr, the youngest son, became the new Kyivan prince.

Under Volodymyr the Great (980–1015) and his son Yaroslav the Wise (1036–1054), Kyivan Rus reached its greatest power. Volodymyr added Galicia-Volhynia, now western Ukraine, to Kyivan Rus. In 988, he converted to Byzantine Christianity in Chersonesus and married a Byzantine princess. Christianity became the official religion of Kyivan Rus. Volodymyr forced his subjects to be baptized into the new religion. Pagan idols of the Slavs were destroyed. Volodymyr supported the new church with 10 percent of his wealth.

Yaroslav became prince after his five brothers died. Under Yaroslav, Kyivan Rus grew to be the largest state in Europe. It reached from the Baltic Sea to the Black Sea and from the Oka River (in present-day Russia) to the Carpathian Mountains.

This drawing commemorates the introduction of Christianity into Kyivan Rus.

Yaroslav developed strong ties with European rulers. His sons married European princesses, and his daughters wed the kings of France, Hungary, and Norway. Yaroslav had 400 golden-domed churches built in Kyiv and also established monasteries. He became known as "the Wise" by organizing a just and fair law code for all of Kyivan Rus. In ancient chronicles written during the eleventh century, the lands around Kyivan Rus were called Ukraine.

The End of Kyivan Rus

After Yaroslav's death, Kyivan Rus began to decline. Yaroslav's sons and nephews divided Kyivan Rus into eight principalities.

Mongols on horseback, from a 14th century Persian manuscript

Each of these large regions of land was ruled by a prince. Much of the trade that had helped build Kyivan Rus stopped as new routes opened through southern Europe to Asia. The Dnipro lost its importance as a trade route, and Kyiv lost its place as a major city.

During the twelfth century, Polovtsian nomads from Central Asia gained control of the steppe. Then in 1222, the Mongols of the Golden Horde began invading Kyivan Rus. Those invaders were called Tatars. Finally, in 1240, Kyiv fell to the Tatars. When Kyivan Rus was securely under their control, the Tatars returned to their homeland on the Volga River.

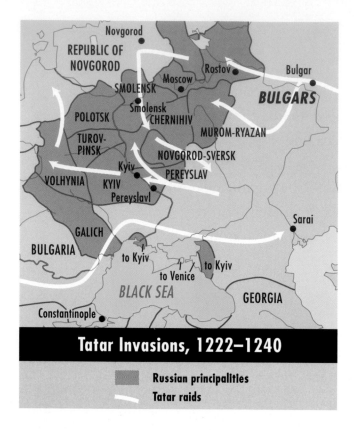

Tatar Invasions, 1222–1240

Russian principalities
Tatar raids

However, the Tatars required the Rus princes to collect tribute for them.

During the long years of invasions, peasant farmers and townspeople from Kyivan Rus began moving into what is now western Ukraine. They found refuge from the invaders in the forests and mountains. The far western principality of Galicia-Volhynia rose to power under Prince Danylo (1238–1264) and his son Lev (1264–1301). As long as they paid tribute, including slaves, the Tatars left them alone. Trade routes linked Galicia-Volhynia with Poland, Hungary, and cities along the Baltic and Black Seas. The capital city of Halych became the center of the salt trade. Later, the new capital Lviv, named for Prince Lev, also became a trading center. In 1303, Halych became the seat of the Orthodox church. By the mid 1300s, however, the ruling family of Galicia-Volhynia had died out.

Lithuanian and Polish Rule

Ukraine's neighboring states of Lithuania and Poland began to move in. By 1380, the grand duke of Lithuania controlled most of what is now Ukraine. The Tatars, however, still dominated the eastern steppe and Krym. In 1380, the grand duke divided Galicia-Volhynia with Poland. Volhynia became part of the

Grand Duchy of Lithuania, and Galicia became part of the Kingdom of Poland. In 1569, Poland and Lithuania were united politically as the Polish-Lithuanian Commonwealth. Through that union, Lithuania's Ukrainian lands came under Polish rule.

Under the Tatars and Lithuanians, few changes occurred to daily life in Ukraine. But Polish rule brought great changes. Polish nobles gained large estates in Ukraine. Many Polish traders, merchants, and craftspeople moved into Ukraine's cities. They brought the Roman Catholic religion and Polish language with them. To maintain their status, many Ukrainian nobles converted from Orthodoxy to Catholicism. They also adopted the Polish language. Non-Catholic Ukrainian townspeople lost their rights to take part in town government. Ukraine's free peasant farmers were made serfs, forced to work the land of a nobleman and not allowed to leave that land. However, the peasants kept the Ukrainian language and Orthodox religion alive.

In the 1596 Union of Brest, some Orthodox bishops declared the union of Ukraine's Orthodox church with the Roman Catholic Church. This union formed the Uniate Church, today called the Ukrainian Catholic Church. The bishops recognized the pope as head of Ukraine's Uniate Church. Church services and ceremonies remained Orthodox and were said in Slavonic. The Union of Brest outlawed the Orthodox Church.

Age of the Kozaks

Many Ukrainian peasants and nobles opposed the way of life under Polish rule. In the 1500s, they fled to empty land in the

Kozaks in the 17th Century

/// Area of unrest

A statue of Bohdan Khmelnytsky in a Kyiv city park

southeastern steppe. These men were called *Kozaks*, a Turkish word for "freemen" or "adventurers." The Kozaks banded together and elected a *rada*, or council. The rada chose a leader called the *hetman*. The Kozaks built fortifications called *siches* on islands in the Dnipro River. Their largest sich was at Zaporizhzhya, which means "beyond the rapids." The Kozaks called themselves the "Zaporizhzhyan Host." Their main missions were to protect Ukraine from foreign invaders and to uphold the Orthodox Church. Through their efforts, the Orthodox leadership was restored to Kyiv in 1620.

Before the Kozaks arrived on the steppe, the power of the Golden Horde had collapsed. Tatars still controlled Krym, but they owed allegiance to Ottoman Turks who had conquered the Byzantine Empire in 1453. The Kozaks led many raids against Turkish cities on the Black Sea. They also protected Polish Ukraine from Tatar attacks.

However, in 1648, Hetman Bohdan Khmelnytsky led the Kozaks with Tatar allies against Poland. He successfully brought most of central and eastern Ukraine under Kozak control. In 1649, Khmelnytsky formed a Kozak state in central Ukraine. When the conflict with Poland continued, Khmelnytsky made an alliance with the Russian tsar in 1654.

Khmelnytsky died in 1657, but warfare and invasions continued across Ukraine until 1667. In that year, Russia and Poland divided Ukraine between them. Land west of the Dnipro River went to Poland; land to the east went to Russia.

The Kozak state, or *hetmanate*, maintained self-government even though it was under the rule of Russian tsar Peter I. Hetman Ivan Mazepa (1687–1709) wanted to create an independent Ukrainian state. In 1708, he formed an alliance with the tsar's enemy Charles XII of Sweden. At the Battle of Poltava in 1709, Peter the Great's army defeated the Kozak and Swedish forces. Russia's rulers eliminated the Hetmanate but kept the Zaporizhzhya Sich in place. It served as a buffer

The Battle of Poltava

against the Ottoman Empire. In 1774, the Russian army of Catherine II defeated the Ottomans and gained their land in southern Ukraine. In 1775, Russian troops destroyed the sich. The era of a Ukrainian state under the Kozaks ended.

Ukraine Under the Russian and Austrian Empires

By the 1770s, Poland had become a weakened state. Prussia (part of what is now Germany), Austria, and Russia divided Poland among themselves. That meant that Ukraine was also divided. In 1772, Austria gained Galicia. In 1793, Russia gained most of Poland's remaining land west of the Dnipro River. In 1795, Volhynia came under Russian control. The Ukrainian lands of Bukovina and Transcarpathia also became part of the Austrian Empire. In 1783, Catherine II annexed the Krymian Peninsula to Russia. All of present-day Ukraine was then held by Russia and Austria.

Life for Ukrainians improved under Austrian rule. Polish nobles in Ukraine kept their land, but serfdom ended. Elementary schools that taught in the Ukrainian language opened. The University of Lviv was founded, although classes were in German. Ukrainians published books and newspapers in their own

Queen Catherine II

language. Cities that had declined under Polish rule began to prosper. Ukrainians who lived in cities received equal rights with Poles and Germans. The Uniate church acknowledged its roots in Byzantine Greece and was renamed the Greek Catholic Church. It was treated as the equal of the Roman Catholic Church. In 1848, revolutions broke out in Europe, including the Austrian Empire. Ukrainians asked for a recognized territory in the empire separate from the Poles, the right to vote, and a Ukrainian university. Instead, the Polish upper class received more power. As a result, thousands of Ukrainians emigrated from Galicia. Many went to Canada and the United States.

Many changes also occurred in the Russian part of Ukraine. The southern and eastern steppe was settled by landowners and peasant farmers. They came from other parts of Ukraine as well as from Russia, Germany, Bulgaria, and other parts of eastern Europe. Cities grew and prospered along the Black Sea and Sea of Azov. Jewish traders and merchants and Armenians and Greeks started businesses in Odesa, Mykolayiv, and Mariupol. Coal mining started in the Donets Basin. Factories opened in nearby towns. Russians flocked to these cities for jobs. Modern universities opened in Kharkiv, Kyiv, and Odesa.

The Ukrainian people, however, fared poorly under Russian rule. Russia regarded Ukraine as a long-lost part of its empire. Russia referred to Ukraine as "Little Russia" and to Ukrainians as "Little Brothers." From 1783 to 1861, Ukraine's peasants, like those in Russia, were enserfed. The Uniate church was outlawed, and Ukrainians were forced into the

Russian Orthodox church. In 1863 and 1876, the Russian government outlawed publication of works in the Ukrainian language. Ukrainian could not be taught in the schools. In the early 1900s, Ukrainian university students formed groups that wanted a free and independent Ukraine.

The Ukrainian National Republic

During World War I (1914–1918), Russia and Austria were on opposing sides. Ukraine, especially Galicia, became a battleground between the two empires. In 1917, a revolution broke out in Russia. Bolsheviks, later called Communists, overthrew the tsar's government and killed the tsar and his family. Politically active Ukrainians used Russia's troubles as a chance to set up a Ukrainian government. Between 1917 and 1921, Ukraine had four different governments that proclaimed an independent Ukrainian National Republic. During these same years, Ukrainian, Bolshevik, anti-Bolshevik, and Polish armies fought to control Ukraine.

Ukraine's republic failed. Its leaders lacked political experience and could not keep its army organized. The uneducated Ukrainian peasants did not understand the republic's goals and so did not support it. In the end, Ukraine was parceled out among four countries. Romania annexed Bukovina. Czechoslovakia gained Transcarpathia. Poland once more claimed Galicia and Volhynia. Soviet Russia received the rest of Ukraine—most of Ukraine's land that had belonged to the Russian Empire. Soviet Ukraine was called the Ukrainian Soviet Socialist Republic.

In 1922, Soviet Ukraine became part of the newly formed Union of Soviet Socialist Republics (USSR). The Communist Party in Moscow, Russia, made all the decisions for the USSR. It also appointed all the government leaders in Ukraine. Under Vladimir Lenin, the USSR's first leader, Ukraine's economy revived after the years of war. Lenin encouraged schools to use the Ukrainian language and promoted the publication of materials in Ukrainian. The Ukrainian Autocephalous Orthodox Church was founded in 1921 as a church independent of the Russian Orthodox Church. *Autocephalous* means "independent." Since it was separate from the Russian Orthodox Church, many Ukrainian peasants joined this church.

Vladimir Lenin (left) with Joseph Stalin

With Lenin's death in 1924, Joseph Stalin became head of the USSR. Stalin wanted to bring the USSR quickly up to the military and industrial level of Europe. To accomplish that goal, Stalin needed the Ukrainian people and their natural resources. Thousands of Ukrainian peasants were moved off the land to become miners and factory workers. To make up for the smaller farm population, Stalin began collectivizing Ukraine's farms in 1929. Farmers had to give up their land, cattle, and farm tools and combine them with those of other farmers. Rather than take part in collectivization, many farmers killed their cattle and destroyed their tools and crops. For punishment, Stalin seized the remaining crops, cattle, and seed. Farmers were not allowed to keep even enough to feed their families. In 1932–1933, about 7 million Ukrainian peasants starved to death. Millions of others were removed from the land and exiled to Kazakhstan and Siberia, where many more died. Stalin sent Russian peasants to work on collective farms in Ukraine.

Also in the 1930s, Stalin clamped down on Ukrainian culture. About 80 percent of Ukraine's artists and writers were arrested, exiled, or put to death. The Ukrainian Autocephalous Orthodox church was shut down. Russian became the official language, and classes were no longer taught in Ukrainian. Stalin even executed Ukrainians who were leaders in Ukraine's Communist Party. He replaced them with Russians. One of them was Nikita Khrushchev.

World War II

World War II started in 1939 when German troops marched into Poland. That year, Ukraine again became a battleground when Soviet troops moved into Polish-held Ukraine. Two years later, troops from Nazi Germany began battling east across Ukraine toward Russia. By the end of 1944, the Soviet army had pushed the Germans from Ukraine. At the war's end in 1945, Ukraine's farms, cities, factories, and roads lay in ruins. About 8 million Ukrainians died during the war. Nazi forces killed more than 600,000 Jews in Ukraine. They also shipped more than 2 million Ukrainians to Germany, where they worked for German companies as slave laborers.

Through the peace treaties that ended World War II, the Soviets gained the rest of western Ukraine—Galicia, Volhynia, Transcarpathia, and Bukovina. Stalin immediately moved to tighten Soviet control over western Ukraine. Farms were collectivized. The Ukrainian Greek Catholic Church was abolished. Many western Ukrainians disagreed with Stalin's policies. About 500,000 of them were arrested and sent to other parts of the Soviet Union.

A woman weeps at the site of her destroyed home.

From "The Thaw" to Glasnost

With Stalin's death in 1953, Nikita Khrushchev became head of the Communist Party and leader of the Soviet Union. He had been head of the Ukrainian Communist Party (1938–1949) after Stalin executed its Ukrainian leaders.

The Race to Space

During the 1950s and 1960s, the United States and the Soviet Union were in a race to space. Both countries wanted to be the first to put a human in space and to land on the moon. The Soviet Union's space program took the lead because of the talents and efforts of Sergei Korolov (1906–1966). Korolov was a rocket engineer born and raised in Zhytomyr, Ukraine. He headed the Soviet space program from 1955 until 1966. Korolov designed the first Soviet guided missiles and spacecrafts. Under his direction in 1957, the Soviet Union launched Sputnik I into earth's orbit. This was the world's first unmanned satellite. Four years later Korolov chose Yuri Gagarin to become the first person in space. Under Korolov's leadership, the Soviet space program enjoyed many more firsts. By the time of Korolov's death in 1966, the U.S. space program had pulled ahead of the Soviets. The first people on the moon were U.S. astronauts, whose lunar landing awed the world in 1969. Since then, however, Ukrainians have continued to play an important role in space exploration. Svitlana Savytska (left) became the first woman to walk in space in 1984. From November 19 to December 5, 1997, cosmonaut Leonid Kadenyuk (right) conducted experiments on plants aboard the U.S. space shuttle *Columbia*.

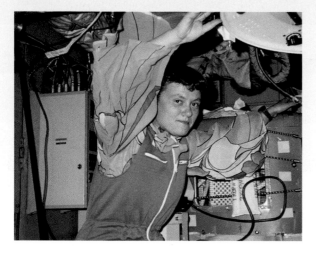 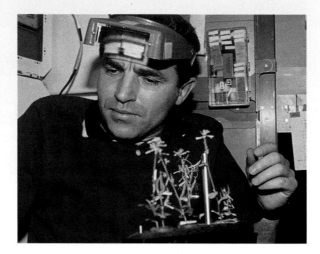

Throughout the Soviet Union's republics, Khrushchev began a policy called "The Thaw" under which the republics gained some control over their own governments and economies. A Ukrainian, Oleksy Kyrychenko, became head of the Ukrainian Communist Party. Ukraine's industries continued to grow.

Some factories started to make consumer goods. In 1954, Khrushchev turned over the Krymian Peninsula to Ukraine. He also allowed Ukrainian artists and writers more freedom of expression. Khrushchev was removed from power in 1964.

The new leaders in Moscow put an end to local government control of the economy. Ukraine's industrial growth slowed down. Farm production had never fully recovered after World War II, and in the 1970s and 1980s, it fell further behind. In fact, the economy of the entire Soviet Union was in bad shape. Mikhail Gorbachev became the Soviet Union's leader in 1985. He started *perestroika*, a program for economic reform. To achieve reform, Gorbachev called for *glasnost*—open and honest discussion.

Under *glasnost*, Ukrainians formed environmental, cultural, and political groups. They brought up issues that convinced many Ukrainians to push for independence. The

Demonstrators in Kyiv, 1990

Green Party worked to close Ukraine's nuclear power plants, especially the one at Chornobyl. Leaders of the Ukrainian Catholic and Ukrainian Autocephalous Orthodox churches asked that their churches be legalized. Ukrainian writers and teachers led the drive to make Ukrainian the official language. Political groups held anti-Communist demonstrations in Lviv and Kyiv in 1988. At that time, the Communist Party was the only legal political party. In 1989, the People's Front of Ukraine for Reconstruction (RUKH) was formed in Kyiv. In the 1990 elections for the Ukrainian Supreme Council, RUKH candidates gained 25 percent of the seats. In October 1990, RUKH began working for complete Ukrainian independence. When the Soviet government in Moscow collapsed in August 1991, the way for independence opened.

Voting in the first presidential election, 1991

Independent Ukraine

On August 24, 1991, the Ukrainian legislature declared Ukraine an independent nation. In a special election on December 1, 1991, 84 percent of Ukraine's eligible voters cast their votes. An overwhelming 90 percent of them voted for an independent Ukraine. They wanted a better life than they had as part of the Soviet Union. On December 1, Ukrainians also voted for a president for the first time. Six candidates from different parties ran for election. Leonid Kravchuk emerged as the winner. He

appointed Leonid Kuchma as prime minister. Both men wanted to work toward a free market economy. The Parliament, still controlled by Communists, voted to block reforms. Kuchma resigned, and Kravchuk returned to state-controlled measures. In the 1994 presidential election, Kuchma defeated Kravchuk. Throughout the rest of the 1990s, Ukraine's economy continued to decline. Nevertheless, Ukrainians voted Kuchma a second term as president in 1999.

Ukrainian President Leonid Kuchma meets with U.S. President Bill Clinton, 1996.

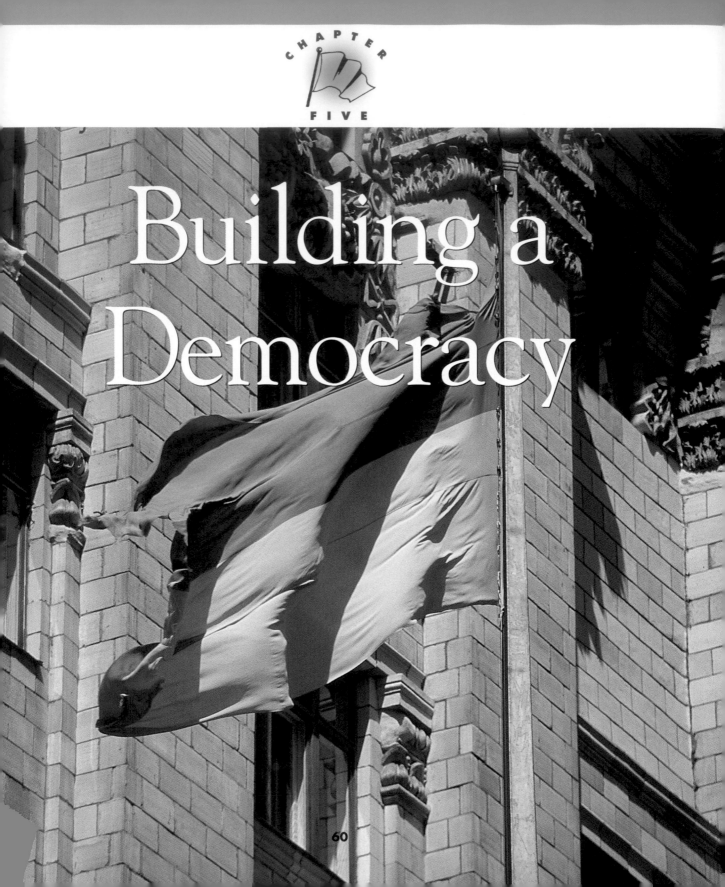

Building a Democracy

FOR THE FIRST TIME SINCE THE END OF KYIVAN RUS, Ukraine is united as an independent nation. Once again, Ukraine is the largest country in Europe. For the first time in its history, Ukraine is also a democratic nation. The Ukrainian people vote in multiparty elections for Ukraine's president, for deputies in the national legislature, and for government officials at the local level.

In 1996, the legislature adopted independent Ukraine's first Constitution. Like the U.S. Constitution, it established three branches of government. The president heads the executive branch. A one-house legislature called the Supreme Council is the legislative branch. The judicial branch is made up of Ukraine's courts. Ukraine's Constitution also lists the country's national symbols; they are the national flag, the national state coat of arms, which is the trident, and the national anthem.

Opposite: **The Ukrainian flag outside a government building**

Ukraine's National Flag

In 1992, Ukraine's government adopted a flag with two equal horizontal stripes. The top stripe is azure blue, and the bottom one is yellow. Kyivan Rus princes, Kozak leaders, and the Ukrainian National Republic used these colors on flags and banners. Blue stands for Ukraine's skies and waters, and yellow represents its fields of wheat and sunflowers.

Ukraine's National Anthem

Ukraine's national anthem expresses the Ukrainian people's love of freedom and acknowledges the need to fight to make Ukraine free. The anthem started as a patriotic Ukrainian poem in 1863. In that year, the Russian tsar abolished serfdom, and Ukrainians longed to be a self-governing people. The poem was set to music later.

"Ukraine Lives On" (*Shche Ne Vmerla Ukrayina*)
Ukraine lives on, so too its glory and freedom,
Good fortune will still smile on us, brother Ukrainians.
Our enemies will die, as the dew does in the sunshine,
and we, too brothers, we'll live happily in our land.

We'll not spare either our souls or bodies to get freedom
and we'll prove that we are brothers of Kozak kin.

We'll rise up, brothers, all of us, from the Syan River to the Don,
We won't let anyone govern in our motherland.
The Black Sea will smile, and grandfather Dnipro will rejoice,
In our Ukraine good fortune will yet abound.

Our persistence, our sincere toil will prove its rightness,
still our freedom's loud song will spread throughout Ukraine.
It'll resound upon the Carpathians, and sound through the steppes,
while Ukraine's glory will arise among the people.

The National Government

The three branches of Ukraine's government have specific powers, and Ukraine's Constitution provides a system of checks and balances among the three branches. The Supreme Council, or *Verkhovna Rada*, is Ukraine's lawmaking body. It has 450 deputies who serve four-year terms. Ukraine's voters directly elect 225 deputies from 225 single-seat districts. The other 225 deputies are proportionately selected from political parties who received at least 4 percent of the vote. For example, if Green Party candidates received 4 percent of the votes cast, that party would gain 9 more seats in the Supreme Council. The Constitution grants the Supreme Council thirty-six specific powers. Among them are the power to make all laws for Ukraine, to approve the national budget, to approve the president's selection of a prime minister, to appoint one-third of the members of the Constitutional Court, and to declare war upon the president's suggestion.

Ukraine's president is the country's chief executive. Ukraine's voters directly elect the president for a five-year term. Ukraine's president is limited to two terms of office. To be president, a person must be thirty-five years old, have lived in Ukraine for ten years, and be able to speak and write the Ukrainian language. Ukraine's Constitution grants the president thirty-one specific powers. Some of the more important powers are appointing the prime minister with the consent of the Supreme Council, and appointing members of the Cabinet of Ministers upon the suggestion of the prime minister. The president is also commander-in-chief of the armed forces, appoints one-third of the members of the Constitutional Court, can establish other courts, and signs laws passed by the Supreme Council. The president, through the Cabinet of Ministers, carries out Ukraine's laws.

Ukraine's First Presidents

Ukraine has held three presidential elections and has elected two presidents and reelected one since becoming an independent nation in 1991. Ukraine's first democratically elected president was Leonid Kravchuk, who held office from December 1991 to July 1994. Born in Velyky Zhytyn in 1934, Kravchuk joined  the Communist Party in 1958. While teaching at the university in Chernivtsi, Kravchuk rose through party ranks and in 1990 became chair of the Ukrainian Supreme Soviet (the Ukrainian Soviet Socialist Republic's legislature). This post made him the leader of Ukraine. When the government of the Soviet Union collapsed, Kravchuk supported independence for Ukraine and left the Communist Party. In the 1994 presidential elections, Leonid Kuchma defeated President Kravchuk because he had not reformed the economy.

Kuchma, born in Chernihiv in 1938, has a degree in mechanical engineering. From 1986 to 1992, he served as director of the world's largest rocket construction company. In 1990, he was elected to the Ukrainian Supreme Soviet. Kuchma also supported independence for Ukraine in 1991 and left the Communist Party. As Ukraine's president, Kuchma has worked to privatize land and businesses, to reduce government corruption, and to improve relations with Russia through free trade. He was elected to a second term in 1999.

Under the tsars and the Soviets, justice was dispensed by rulers or by their secret police. To protect the Ukrainian people from that kind of "justice," the Constitution states that only the courts will administer justice. The Ukrainian people take part in the administration of justice as jurors. The Supreme Court is Ukraine's highest court for nonconstitutional issues. Its judges are appointed by the Supreme Council for permanent terms. Courts of appeal and local courts are under the Supreme Court. Unlike the U.S. Supreme Court, Ukraine's Supreme Court does not rule on the constitutionality of laws. Instead, the Constitutional Court of Ukraine interprets

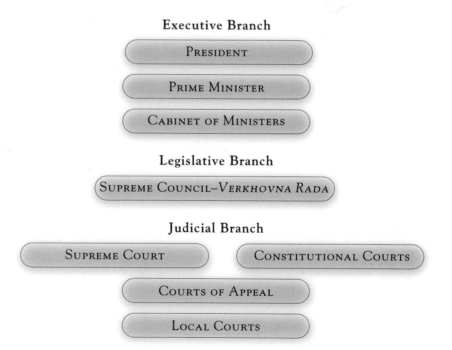

NATIONAL GOVERNMENT OF UKRAINE

Executive Branch

PRESIDENT

PRIME MINISTER

CABINET OF MINISTERS

Legislative Branch

SUPREME COUNCIL–VERKHOVNA RADA

Judicial Branch

SUPREME COURT   CONSTITUTIONAL COURTS

COURTS OF APPEAL

LOCAL COURTS

the Constitution and decides whether laws passed by the Supreme Council agree with the Constitution. The Constitutional Court has eighteen judges. Ukraine's president, Supreme Council, and Congress of Judges each appoints six judges. They are appointed for a nine-year term and cannot be reappointed.

Local Government

Ukraine is divided into twenty-four regions called *oblasts* and one autonomous republic. Each oblast has a capital that is named for the oblast. For example, Ternopil is the capital of Ternopil Oblast. This rule does not apply, however, to two oblasts. The capital of Volyn Oblast is Lutsk; that of Zakarpattya Oblast is Uzhhorod. The oblasts are further divided in *rayons*, or counties. Each oblast and rayon has a legislative council and an executive. Cities, villages, and towns have councils and mayors. At each level of local government, the officials are directly elected by voters. Local councils vote on programs that improve the social, economic, and cultural life of their area. They also levy taxes and approve budgets to fund those programs.

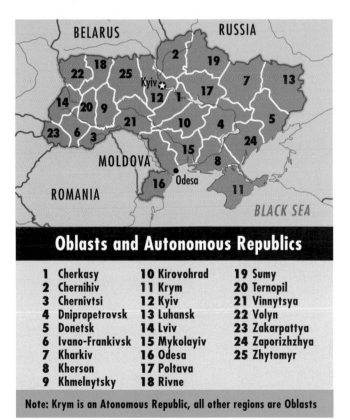

Oblasts and Autonomous Republics

1 Cherkasy	10 Kirovohrad	19 Sumy
2 Chernihiv	11 Krym	20 Ternopil
3 Chernivtsi	12 Kyiv	21 Vinnytsya
4 Dnipropetrovsk	13 Luhansk	22 Volyn
5 Donetsk	14 Lviv	23 Zakarpattya
6 Ivano-Frankivsk	15 Mykolayiv	24 Zaporizhzhya
7 Kharkiv	16 Odesa	25 Zhytomyr
8 Kherson	17 Poltava	
9 Khmelnytsky	18 Rivne	

Note: Krym is an Atonomous Republic, all other regions are Oblasts

The Parliament and Ministry Building, Simferopol

Krym, also known as Crimea, is an autonomous republic within Ukraine. Its capital is Simferopol. The majority of people in Krym are ethnic Russians. In the mid-1990s, they pushed to leave Ukraine and rejoin Russia. The Krymian government wrote a constitution that was for independence and included a Krymian president. Ukraine's Supreme Council abolished that constitution and the office of president. Krym now has a Constitution that was approved by Ukraine's Supreme Council. All of Krym's laws must be in line with Ukraine's Constitution. Krym also has a Supreme Council and prime minister. The prime minister is appointed by the Supreme Council with the approval of Ukraine's Supreme Council.

Voters, Political Parties, and Elections

Ukraine has about 38,500,000 registered voters in a population of about 50,500,000. All citizens of Ukraine who have reached eighteen years of age may vote. Ukraine's election laws require that at least 50 percent of eligible voters take part in an election. Ukrainians take their right and duty to vote seriously. In the 1999 presidential election, about 74 percent of registered voters turned out.

About thirty political parties have nationwide support in Ukraine. They range from the extreme right Congress of Ukrainian Nationalists to the far left Ukrainian Communist Party. In between are parties such as RUKH and the Green Party.

Candidates from the Communist Party won the most seats in both the 1994 and 1998 Supreme Council elections. To win an election, a candidate must receive a majority (at least 51 percent) of the vote. Because so many parties field candidates, a second election between the highest two vote-getters is usually necessary to gain a majority vote.

Ukraine's elections for the most part have been free, open, and democratic. During the 1999 presidential campaign, however, President Kuchma's opponents accused him of tampering with the news media. Members of the Verkhovna Rada stated that Kuchma had forced the government to suppress his opponents and raise funds for his reelection. Ukrainian crowds became rowdy at several campaign rallies, with violence erupting at one of

Casting ballots in the 1999 presidential election

them. A bomb was thrown at Natalya Vitrenko, the Progressive Socialist Party candidate. Luckily, she was not seriously injured.

Foreign Affairs

Ukraine was one of the original members of the United Nations (UN). Soviet Ukraine received a permanent seat in the General Assembly as a compromise with the Soviet Union. The Soviets had wanted seats for all fifteen of its republics. Since then, Ukraine has also held a two-year temporary seat in the Security Council three times: 1948–1949, 1984–1985, and 2000–2001.

The Livadiya Palace

Yalta, a Black Sea resort city in southern Krym, has attracted vacationers since the nineteenth century. Nicholas II, Russia's last tsar, built the Livadiya Palace as a summer retreat for his family in 1910. During World War II, the palace was the site of the Yalta Conference. Joseph Stalin of the USSR, U.S. president Franklin D. Roosevelt, and British prime minister Winston Churchill met there in February 1945. They decided to divide Germany at the end of World War II. Also at that conference, Roosevelt and Churchill agreed that the USSR's western border should include the eastern lands of Poland—western Ukraine. In 1999, President Kuchma held his meeting with Baltic and Black Sea leaders at the Livadiya Palace.

Leaders join hands at the 1999 Yalta meeting, Livadiya Palace

As a UN member, Ukraine has always voted for peaceful, negotiated settlements to worldwide disputes. It sent troops to serve in Bosnia with UN peace-keeping forces.

Since its independence, Ukraine has increased its ties to the West. In 1992, Ukraine joined the Organization for Security and Cooperation in Europe. In 1994, it signed an agreement for partnership and cooperation with the European Union (EU), and in 1994, it joined NATO's (North Atlantic Treaty Organization) Partnership for Peace program. Ukraine sent troops to join NATO peacekeeping forces in Kosovo in 1999. Ukraine has also entered into programs with the United States. The United States has sent advisors to show how to hold free elections, how to set up political parties, and how to reform the justice system.

Ukraine has also been a leader in seeking closer ties with its Black Sea and Baltic neighbors. In 1999, President Kuchma hosted a meeting in Yalta of fourteen leaders from Black Sea and Baltic Sea countries. The leaders agreed to start joint programs in environmental protection, transportation, and communication.

Kyiv: Did You Know This?

Kyiv, Ukraine's capital, is also the country's largest city. About 2,600,000 people live there. Founded in A.D. 482, Kyiv served as the capital of Kyivan Rus, the hetmanate, and the Ukrainian National Republic. From 1934 to 1991, Kyiv (also known as Kiev) was the capital of the Ukrainian Soviet Socialist Republic.

Ukraine's capital straddles the Dnipro River. High above the Dnipro's west bank stands a 15-foot- (4.6-m-) tall bronze statue of Volodymyr the Great. Buildings from Kyivan Rus, such as Saint Sophia Cathedral and the Caves Monastery, have survived on the west bank.

The Golden Gate, built by Yaroslav the Wise, was restored in 1982. Colorful buildings stand out in west bank neighborhoods. Saint Andrew's Church has green, gold, and blue cupolas. The red-painted main building of Kyiv University, or Shevchenko University, was destroyed during World War II. It was rebuilt between 1946 and 1952. Buildings that house Ukraine's legislature and the president's offices are also on the west bank. Dozens of museums, in and around the city, highlight Ukrainian art, folk art, religion, history, and natural history.

Land on Kyiv's east bank has miles and miles of huge apartment buildings, most built during the Soviet era. Bridges connect the west bank to the east bank. The Metro Bridge is 2,600 feet (792 m) long. The average daily temperature in Kyiv is 21°F (6°C) in January and 67°F (20°C) in July.

About 2 miles (3.2 km) from the city center is a pretty park. During World War II, this was a ravine called Babyn Yar. Nazi forces killed and buried more than 150,000 Ukrainians, mainly Jews, in the ravine. Today, two monuments honor the dead.

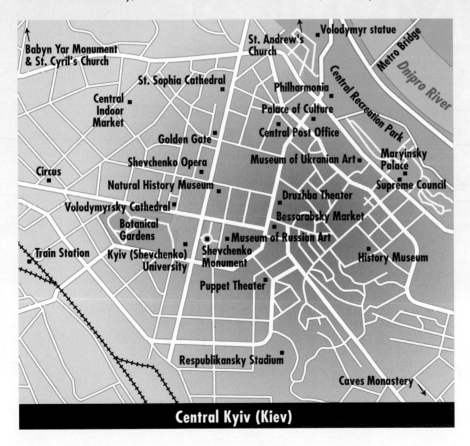

Central Kyiv (Kiev)

Toward a Market Economy

70

ONE REASON UKRAINE DECLARED INDEPENDENCE WAS to reform its economy. Ukraine's new leaders proposed a plan to move to a free market economy. The plan called for privatization, reducing government spending, freeing prices, encouraging foreign investment, and stopping government corruption. Through privatization, the government would sell its mines, factories, and land. Then the new owners would decide what and how much to produce, and they would also set prices. Privatization, however, has moved slowly. Few people have enough money to purchase property. Some businesspeople have entered into joint ventures with foreign companies to purchase government property. However, confusing business laws and high taxes discourage both Ukrainians and foreigners from running businesses.

In 1996, Ukraine's economy had started to stabilize. The government introduced its new currency, the *hryvnia*, and hoped the economy would improve. As Ukraine's government reduced spending and let prices rise, the economy continued to decline. By the end of 1999, Ukraine had a foreign debt equal to U.S.$12 billion. Prices were high. Many factories had closed. About 5 million workers were unemployed. Other workers and retired people hadn't been paid for months. Average wages were equal to U.S.$25 to U.S.$40 a month.

Some Ukrainians were tempted to look back at the Soviet era as good times. Most, however, seemed willing to tough it

Opposite: **Inside a tractor factory**

Ukraine's Historic Currency

Ukraine's monetary unit is the *hryvnia*. Each hryvnia contains 100 *kopiykas*. Bank notes are issued in denominations of 1, 2, 5, 10, 20, 50, and 100 hryvnia. As Ukrainians spend their colorful hryvnia notes, they can learn about Ukraine's history. The portrait of a different political or cultural leader is on the front of each bill. The back of each bill shows a famous building that is connected to the person on the front of the note. The following chart describes the seven denominations of hryvnia notes.

Note	Color	Front of Note	Back of Note	
1	Green	Volodymyr the Great, ruler of Kyivan Rus	Ruins of Chersonesus, Krym; where Volodymyr was baptized	
2	Red-brown	Yaroslav the Wise, ruler of Kyivan Rus	St. Sophia Cathedral, Kyiv; built by Yaroslav	
5	Blue	Bohdan Khmelnytsky, Kozak hetman	Church in Subotiv, Khmelnytsky's home village	
10	Purple	Ivan Mazepa, Kozak hetman	Caves Monastery, Kyiv	
20	Brown	Ivan Franko, writer	Opera House, Lviv	
50	Multicolor	Mykhailo Hrushevsky, president of Ukrainian National Republic	Parliament Building, Kyiv	
100	Multicolor	Taras Shevchenko, poet and artist	St. Sophia Cathedral, Kyiv	

What a Hryvnia Can Buy

Item	Cost in Hryvny (Hr)	U.S. $ Equivalent
Lee jeans	200–240 Hr	$50–60
Shoes	80–600 Hr	$20–150
CD	16–20 Hr	$4–5
Paperback book	8–12 Hr	$2–3
New Ukrainian Tavria car	8,000–12,000 Hr	$2,000–$3,000
Used Ford Escort (10 years old)	12,000–16,000 Hr	$3,000–$4,000
Bicycle	200 Hr	$50
Loaf of bread	60–80 kopiykas	15¢–20¢
Bottle of milk	1–1.5 Hr	25¢–38¢
Ice cream cone	80 kopiykas	20¢
Soda pop	2.40 Hr	60¢
Candy bar	1–1.20 Hr	25¢–30¢
1 liter (0.26 gallons) of gasoline	1.50–3.50 Hr	38¢–88¢

out until the economy became more balanced. They realized it would take time to change from a system that had been in place for about seventy years. In the meantime, about 30 percent of Ukraine's citizens continue to produce goods in manufacturing and mining. Agricultural workers make up about 20 percent of the workforce. And about 50 percent of Ukrainians provide services in the fields of government, trade, education, health care, communication, transportation, and tourism.

Manufacturing

From the end of World War II until 1989, the Soviet Union and the United States engaged in the Cold War. Each country was worried about what the other might do militarily. As a result, both countries spent billions of dollars on defense.

They built up huge arsenals of weapons, rockets, missiles, fighter aircraft, and naval vessels. Ukraine's factories turned out about two-thirds of the Soviet Union's defense products. The world's largest missile plant was Yuzhmash, in Dnipropetrovsk. When the Cold War ended and the Soviet Union collapsed, there was no need for those weapons. Some of Ukraine's defense factories have successfully converted to making peacetime goods. Trolley buses, tractors, motorcycles, and fire engines now roll off their assembly lines. Iron and steel products, as well as heavy equipment for mines and factories, continue to lead Ukraine's manufactured goods.

Rockets are made and assembled in the Yuzhmash missile plant.

Rockets for Peace

In October 1999, Zenit rockets made in the Yuzhmash plant launched a communication satellite into space. This project is called Sea Launch because it took place on a platform in the Pacific Ocean. Sea Launch is a joint venture of the Boeing Company in the United States, Ukraine's Yuzhmash company, a Russian company, and the Norwegian Kvaerner Maritime company. The satellite itself is owned by General Motors, in the United States.

In the shift from defense products, Ukraine's factories are also increasing the amount of consumer goods. More automobiles, refrigerators, television sets, and washing machines are available. Clothing, shoes, and processed foods are also more plentiful.

A Coca-Cola factory in Kyiv

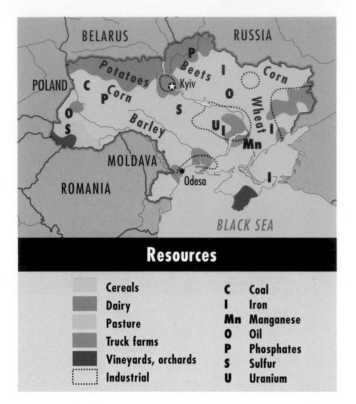

Resources

Cereals		C	Coal
Dairy		I	Iron
Pasture		Mn	Manganese
Truck farms		O	Oil
Vineyards, orchards		P	Phosphates
Industrial		S	Sulfur
		U	Uranium

Horses pull a wagonload of hay on a collective farm in Lviv.

Much of Ukraine's manufacturing revolves around agriculture. Besides tractors, Ukraine's factories make other tools and equipment used on farms. Chemical factories make fertilizers and pesticides to increase the yield of the country's crops. The food-processing industry includes sugar refineries, meat processing and packing plants, fruit and vegetable canneries, dairies, and wineries.

Agriculture

About 20 percent of Ukraine's workers have jobs on farms. If they work on a state farm, they are paid by the government. If they work on a collective farm, they receive wages from the government and also share in their farm's profits. About 2 percent of Ukraine's farms are privately owned. They are the most productive farms in Ukraine. Horse-drawn equipment is still used on many of these farms because individual farmers cannot afford tractors or the gasoline needed to power them.

For about 200 years, Ukraine was called "the breadbasket of Europe" and then "the breadbasket of the

Harvesting strawberries

Soviet Union." Except in years of severe drought, Ukraine's rich, black soil produces high yields of crops. Sugar beets and wheat are the leading steppe crops. Other important grains include barley, corn, oats, rye, millet, and buckwheat. On Ukraine's irrigated southern steppe, melons, peppers, and tomatoes grow well. Rice is grown on Krym's irrigated steppe. Ukraine is one of the world's largest producers of sunflowers, which are mainly grown for their oil. Large crops of potatoes grow in northern Ukraine. Vineyards for wine-making are found in the Carpathian and Krymian Mountains.

Poultry vendors in a Kyiv market

Livestock is raised throughout Ukraine. Chickens, ducks, geese, and turkeys are found on large and small farms. Eggs and meat from these animals add to the Ukrainian diet. Large flocks of sheep graze on grasslands in the Carpathian Mountains and on Krym's steppeland. Beef cattle rove over pastures of northern Ukraine, while dairy cows feed on grasslands close to Ukraine's large cities. Beekeeping remains an important part of Ukrainian agriculture. Bees produce honey and wax.

Mining and Energy

About 400,000 miners work in Ukraine's more than 200 coal mines. They mine anthracite coal in the Donets Basin, bituminous coal in the Dnipro Basin and in northwestern Ukraine, and lignite (brown coal) in the Dnipro Basin. Ukraine's mines fell into disrepair during the Soviet era. Today, they are the most dangerous ones in the world. In March 2000, a methane gas explosion killed 80 miners in Krasnodon in the Donets Basin. This was one of Ukraine's deadliest mining disasters. However, between 1997 and 1999,

Miners in the Donets Basin

almost 900 miners were killed. In 1999, about 13,000 coal miners were injured in mining accidents. Ukraine's miners frequently stage strikes to protest unsafe working conditions and to be paid. Sometimes the government is unable to pay them for up to fifteen months.

Mining of iron ore takes place near Kryvyy Rih, Kremenchuk, Mariupol, and Kerch. One of the world's largest deposits of manganese is near Nicopol. Ukraine's anthracite and bituminous coals are used to heat iron ore and manganese in the steelmaking process. Ukraine's bauxite is made into aluminum. Nickel, titanium, mercury, and salt are also mined in Ukraine.

Coal miners on strike hold a demonstration.

What Ukraine Grows, Makes, and Mines

Agriculture (1996)

Sugar beets	23,009,000 metric tons
Potatoes	18,410,000 metric tons
Wheat	13,547,000 metric tons

Manufacturing (1997)

Rolled ferrous metals	21,000,000 metric tons
Paper	8,700,000 metric tons
Mineral fertilizer	3,900,000 metric tons

Mining

Coal (1994)	91,800,000 metric tons
Iron ore (1996)	48,000,000 metric tons
Manganese (1995)	3,200,000 metric tons

Ukraine has large deposits of petroleum and natural gas, but most of them have not been developed. So Ukraine imports about 80 percent of its oil and 78 percent of its natural gas from Russia. By 1999, Ukraine owed Russia an equivalent of U.S.$1.8 billion for natural gas supplies. To pay down this debt, Ukraine agreed to ship food and manufactured products, including fighter jets, to Russia.

Electricity is another source of energy for Ukraine. Hydroelectric plants at dams along the Dnipro and Southern Buh Rivers supply about 6 percent of Ukraine's electricity. About 43 percent of Ukraine's electricity is produced by plants using coal. Ukraine depends on its nuclear reactors for 47 percent of its electricity. Because of the nuclear explosion at Chornobyl in 1986, independent Ukraine's government agreed to shut down the rest of the Chornobyl reactors by 2000.

A dam at the Dnipro River power plant

Additional reactors were being built at the Rivne and Khmelnytsky nuclear plants. However, by the end of 1999, the new reactors hadn't been completed, and Ukraine decided to keep the reactor at Chornobyl open. Ukraine could not afford to lose the electric power produced by that plant. In December 2000, during an official ceremony, the Chornobyl plant was finally shut down.

Tourism is one of Ukraine's fast-growing service industries. In 1998, about 2 million foreign tourists visited Ukraine. That number had increased sixteen times since 1992. Ukraine earns more than the equivalent of U.S.$200 million a year from tourists. In 1998, about 60,000 people worked in the tourist industry. As this industry grows, many of Ukraine's unemployed will find new ways to earn a living.

Trade is another important service industry. Ukraine's main trading partners are Russia, Turkmenistan, Poland, Germany, and the United States. The main exported goods are sugar beets, wheat, coal, iron goods, chemicals, and construction equipment. Ukraine's main imports are oil, natural gas, rubber, wood products, textiles, and consumer goods. Since Ukraine imports more than it exports, it has a trade deficit—more money is going out than is coming in.

Local vendors offer goods for sale to tourists.

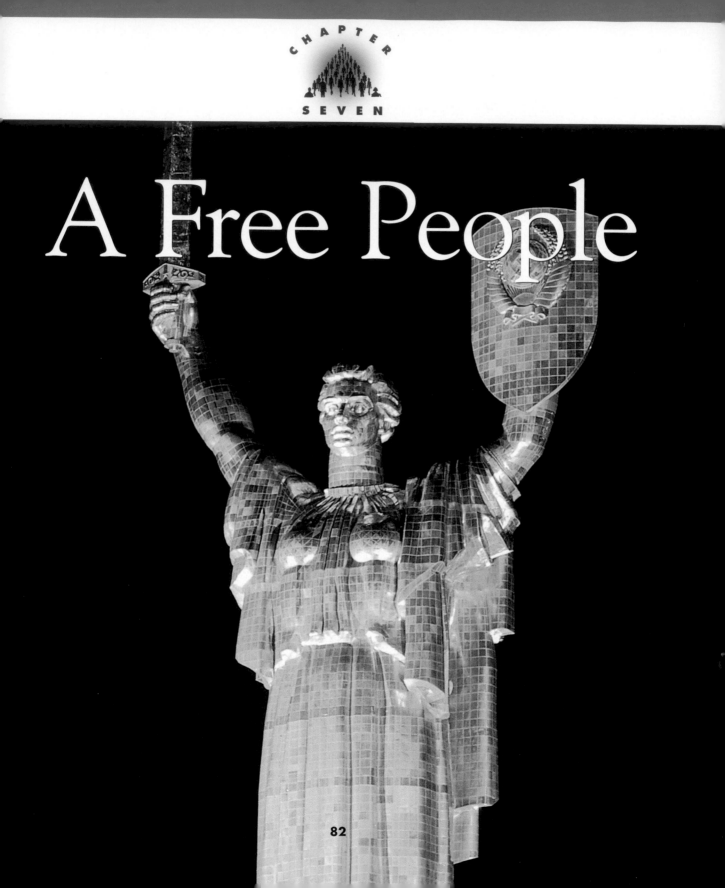

A Free People

OR HUNDREDS OF YEARS, THE UKRAINIAN PEOPLE WERE treated like second-class citizens—first by Poland, then by tsarist Russia, and finally by Soviet Russia. Since its independence, the Ukrainians have used their new-found freedom well. Instead of limiting the rights of ethnic minorities in Ukraine, the Ukrainian government ensures equal rights to all its citizens. Ukraine's Constitution states, "There shall be no privileges or restrictions based on race, color of skin, . . . ethnic and social origin, . . . linguistic or other characteristics."

In the year 2000, 49,811,174 million people lived in Ukraine. That made Ukraine's population the fifth largest in Europe after Germany's, the United Kingdom's, France's, and Italy's. About 71 percent of Ukraine's people live in or near cities. Ukraine's most densely populated area extends from the Donets Basin to just west of the Dnipro River. The other 29 percent of the population live in rural Ukraine. Most of those people live in large villages and work on state-owned or collective farms. Few people live in the marshy forests of northern Ukraine or in the Carpathian and Krymian Mountains.

Population of Major Cities (1998)

City	Population
Kyiv	2,600,000
Donetsk	2,065,000
Kharvkiv	1,521,000
Dnipropetrovsk	1,122,000
Odesa	1,027,000

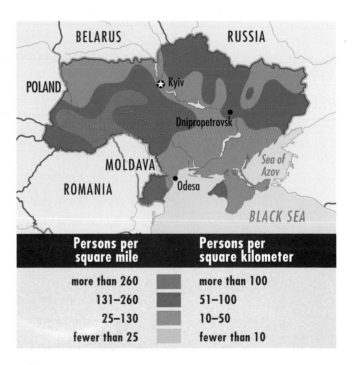

Persons per square mile		Persons per square kilometer
more than 260		more than 100
131–260		51–100
25–130		10–50
fewer than 25		fewer than 10

Travelers from Moscow arrive in Simferopol, Krym.

The People of Ukraine

Ukrainians are the majority population at 73 percent. Large numbers of Ukrainians live in western Ukraine and in rural areas throughout Ukraine. Russians are the largest ethnic minority. They make up 22 percent of Ukraine's population. Eastern cities, especially those in the Donets coal-mining areas, are home to about 80 percent of Ukraine's ethnic Russians. In Krym, ethnic Russians are the majority population. Both the tsars and the Soviets encouraged Russians to move to Ukraine. They provided much needed labor in Ukraine's mines and factories. In the late Soviet era, many Russians retired to Krym because of its warm climate.

People of more than 100 other nationalities also live in Ukraine. Altogether, they make up only 5 percent of the population. The largest of those ethnic minorities come from neighboring Belarus, Moldava, Poland, Hungary, and Romania. The families of many of those people stayed in Ukraine when borders were redrawn after various wars. People of Bulgarian, Greek, Armenian, German, and Tatar backgrounds make up other ethnic groups in Ukraine. Many of these people came to Ukraine as traders and merchants.

The Tatars

The Tatars are a Turkish people who live in Krym. They are descendants of the Tatars who first controlled Krym in the thirteenth century. In 1475, the Tatars became part of the

Ottoman Empire but continued to rule Krym. At the height of their power, the Tatars numbered over 5 million. The Tatars were Muslims—people who practiced the Islamic religion. They built beautiful mosques in which to worship.

Tatar men, Krym

Poland, Russia, and the Kozaks fought the Tatars during the fifteenth through the eighteenth centuries. Finally, in 1783, Catherine the Great annexed Krym to Russia. Thousands of Tatars left Krym and settled in other parts of the Ottoman Empire. By the time of the Russian Revolution in 1917, about 300,000 Tatars remained in Krym. Stalin accused them of helping the Germans during World War II, and in 1944, the remaining Tatars were deported to Siberia and Uzbekistan.

A shantytown in Krym

In 1967, the Soviets cleared the Tatars of Stalin's charges but did nothing to resettle them in Krym. Since the 1980s, the remaining Tatars began returning to Krym. In 1994, several Tatars were elected to the Krymian legislature. Today, about 250,000 Tatars live in Krym. Another 250,000 remain in parts of the former Soviet Union. Several Tatars are deputies in the Krymian legislature, and others serve as ministers in the

Who Lives in Ukraine? (1998)	
Ukrainians	73.0 %
Russians	22.0 %
Belarusians	0.9 %
Moldovans	0.6 %
Tatars	0.5 %
Others	3.0 %

Krymian prime minister's government. However, most Tatars are jobless and live in shantytowns at the edges of Krym's cities. Tatars are helping one another. In 1999, the United Nations Development Program honored Elmaz Alimovna Appazova, a Krymian Tatar. She is a dentist who returned to Krym from Uzbekistan. Appazova helped build a low-cost dental clinic for her fellow returnees.

Ukrainians Abroad

Since the late nineteenth century, hundreds of thousands of Ukrainians have immigrated to other countries. They left Ukraine to escape religious, intellectual, and political persecution. More recently, they have left because of economic hard times. Today, almost 12 million ethnic Ukrainians live outside Ukraine. About 7 million of them live in Russia, and another 2 million live in the United States and Canada. The rest live in Australia, South America, and Western Europe.

Selman Waksman at work in his laboratory, 1943

Two Ukrainians who immigrated to the United States later received Nobel Prizes. In 1952, Selman Waksman, from Pryluki, Ukraine, received the Nobel Prize for Physiology or Medicine. In the 1940s, he had discovered that the antibiotic streptomycin destroyed the bacteria that caused tuberculosis. Simon Kuznets, from Kharkiv, Ukraine, arrived in New York in 1922. An economist, he determined a way of measuring a nation's income. In 1971, he was awarded the Nobel Prize in Economics.

Economist Simon Kuznets

The Ukrainian Language

Ukrainian has been the official language in Ukraine since 1990. Because Russian was the official language of the Soviet Union, many people in Ukraine still speak and write Russian as their first language. This is especially true of people in Ukraine's eastern cities. Ukrainian is the main language in western Ukraine and in most of rural Ukraine. Schools throughout the country have started using Ukrainian instead of Russian as the language of instruction. In this way, all children in Ukraine will grow up learning Ukrainian. A common language will bring people in Ukraine closer to one another. Ukraine's government, however, allows ethnic minorities to continue using their own languages.

Students in Lviv study English in a language lab.

Written Ukrainian looks quite different from English. English, French, and many other European languages are written in Roman letters, or characters. The Ukrainian language, however, is written in Cyrillic characters. The characters in the Cyrillic alphabet are derived from Greek letters. Today, the Belarusian, Bulgarian, Macedonian, Russian, and Serbian languages also use the Cyrillic alphabet.

The Ukrainian alphabet has thirty-three letters. Thirty-two of them have sounds. One of them is a soft sign (ь).

Creating a Language

Cyril (827–869) and Methodius (825–884), brothers from Macedonia, worked as Christian missionaries to the Slavs. In the 860s, they translated the Bible and other sacred works into a language that became known as Church Slavonic. To write Church Slavonic, Cyril and Methodius developed a new alphabet. It became known as the Cyrillic alphabet. As Christianity spread among the Slavs, they began to use Church Slavonic as their written language. When Volodymyr the Great adopted Christianity for Kyivan Rus, Church Slavonic became the language of his princedom. Over many years, the Ukrainian written and spoken language evolved from Church Slavonic. Today, Church Slavonic is still used in church services of some Eastern Orthodox churches.

The Cyrillic Alphabet

The following chart shows the Cyrillic letters in the Ukrainian alphabet, their English equivalent letters, and their Ukrainian pronunciation.

Ukrainian Letters	English Letters	Pronunciation	Ukrainian Letters	English Letters	Pronunciation
А а	A a	like *a* in father	Н н	N n	like *n* in no
Б б	B b	like *b* in bat	О о	O o	like *o* in off
В в	V v	like *v* in very	П п	P p	like *p* in pet
Г г	H h	like *h* in hat and *g* in goat	Р р	R r	like *r* in roof
Ґ ґ	G g	like *g* in got	С с	S s	like *s* in sorry
Д д	D d	like *d* in day	Т т	T t	like *t* in tight
Е е	E e	like *e* in end	У у	U u	like *oo* in root
Є є	YE ye	like *ye* in yes	Ф ф	F f	like *f* in fame
Ж ж	ZH zh	like *ge* in rouge or *s* in measure	Х х	KH kh	like *kh* in khan
З з	Z z	like *z* in zoo	Ц ц	TS ts	like *ts* in rats
И и	Y y	like *i* in milk or *y* in myth	Ч ч	CH ch	like *ch* in cheese
І і	I i	like *ee* in meet	Ш ш	SH sh	like *sh* in shoe
Ї ї	YI yi	like *yie* in yield	Щ щ	SHCH shch	like *shch* in fresh cheese
Й й	Y y	like *y* in yolk	ь		soft sign
К к	K k	like *k* in kind	Ю ю	YU yu	like the word *you* or the *u* in unit
Л л	L l	like *l* in land	Я я	YA ya	like *ya* in yacht or in young
М м	M m	like *m* in mama	'		apostrophe that follows some consonants and softens them

It softens the consonant that precedes it. In some ways, Ukrainian is easier than English. For example, there is only one stressed or accented syllable per word, no matter how long the word is. However, there is no pattern for accents or stresses in Ukrainian. The stress may fall on any syllable in a word.

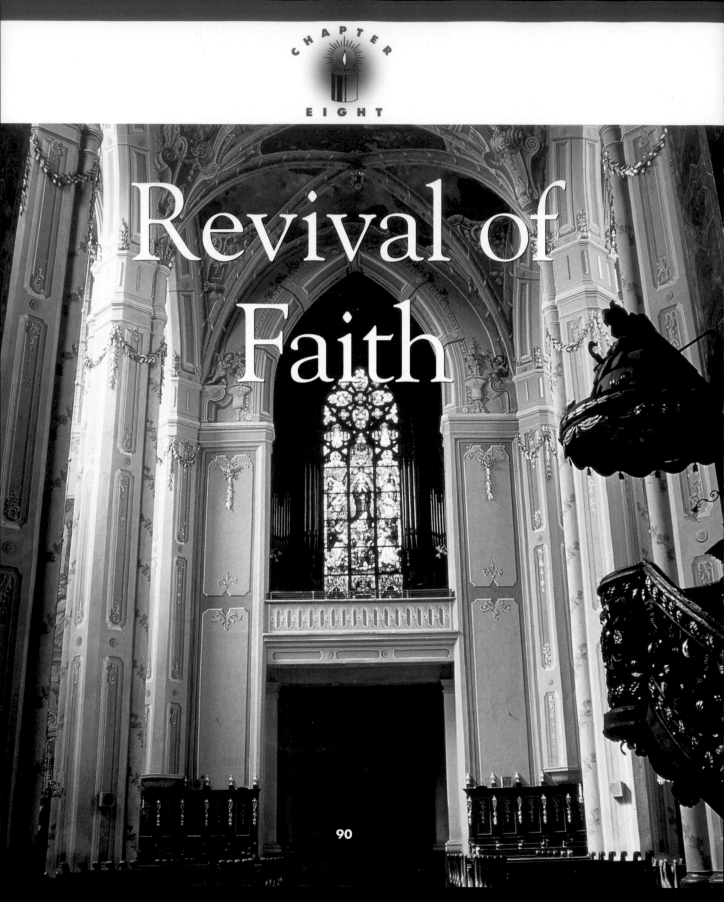

Revival of Faith

During the Soviet era, the Russian Orthodox Church was the only religion allowed. However, people were discouraged from practicing even that religion. The Soviets closed churches, mosques, synagogues, and other religious buildings throughout Ukraine. Some became museums. Others were used as warehouses or simply abandoned. Joseph Stalin had about 250 houses of worship destroyed. In fact, Saint Sophia's Cathedral in Kyiv was saved only because of an outcry from other countries.

Communist thought guided all phases of life in the Soviet Union, including Ukraine. Soviet Communism stated that there was no God, and that governments only allowed religion so people wouldn't think about how miserable they were. Many Ukrainians, however, continued to practice their faiths in secret.

During *glasnost* in the 1980s, Ukrainians brought religion back into the open. In 1988, they celebrated 1,000 years of Christianity. They dated the beginning of Christianity in Ukraine to the year when Volodymyr the Great was baptized. Believers and clergy of the Ukrainian Catholic Church and Ukrainian Autocephalous Orthodox Church gained legal status for their churches. Leaders of these denominations reopened many churches. Some churches were rebuilt or restored, and new churches and synagogues are being built.

Opposite: **Interior of a cathedral, Lviv**

An Orthodox priest outside a newly rebuilt church

A Jewish student reading, Kyiv

Ukraine's new Constitution grants freedom of religion and separates church matters from the state. By the year 2000, most Ukrainians said they belonged to a church or believed in a religion. About 35 million Ukrainians belong to the Ukrainian Orthodox Church. The Ukrainian Catholic Church has about 5 million members, mainly in western Ukraine. About 500,000 Jews live mainly in Kyiv, Lviv, and Odesa. Krym's 250,000 Tatars are Muslims. About 500,000 Poles and Hungarians in Ukraine are Roman Catholics. Since its independence, Protestant churches in the United States and Canada have sent missionaries to Ukraine. Today, there are about 2 million Baptists, Lutherans, Methodists, and Mormons in Ukraine.

Ukrainian Orthodoxy

Religions of Ukraine (1995)	
Ukrainian Orthodox	70 %
Ukrainian Catholic	10 %
Protestant	4 %
Roman Catholic	1 %
Jewish	1 %
Muslim	0.5 %
Other (mostly nonreligious)	13.5 %

By the end of the 1990s, there were three branches of the Ukrainian Orthodox Church. One branch had been the Russian Orthodox Church in Ukraine. The head of this branch is the patriarch of Moscow. Another Ukrainian Orthodox branch has as its leader the patriarch of Kyiv. Plus, the Ukrainian Autocephalous Orthodox branch has its own patriarch, also in Kyiv. All three churches share the same beliefs, hold the same kinds of services, and observe the same holy days. Many Ukrainian Orthodox would like to see the three branches united as one Ukrainian Orthodox Church.

As Christians, the Orthodox believe that Jesus Christ is the Son of God and that he is the Redeemer of mankind. The Orthodox also believe that Mary was the mother of Jesus and that the saints can intervene between people and Jesus.

Orthodox priests may be married before they take their vows. Bishops cannot be married. Orthodox ceremonies are conducted in the Ukrainian language, but music is sung or chanted in Old Church Slavonic. The human voice is the only musical instrument allowed during Orthodox ceremonies. Worshipers must stand or kneel during Orthodox services because the churches do not have pews or chairs. However, some of the newer churches provide seating.

Orthodox priests conduct a Christmas service.

Worshipers approach the altar at St. George's Cathedral, Lviv.

Today's Ukrainian Catholic Church is the descendant of the Uniate Church formed in 1596. The Ukrainian Catholic Church has the same ceremonies and rites and rituals as the Ukrainian Orthodox Church. Its priests also can be married. The only difference is that the pope is the head of the church and appoints bishops. When the Soviet government legalized the Ukrainian Catholic Church, Pope John Paul II appointed ten bishops. The metropolitan, or head, of the Ukrainian Catholic Church once again presides over that church from Saint George's Cathedral in Lviv.

Metropolitan Andrei Sheptytsky, Ukrainian Hero

During World War II, the leader of the Ukrainian Catholic Church became a great hero. Andrei Sheptytsky, born in the Lviv region in 1865, became a priest in 1892. Just eight years later, he was named metropolitan of the Ukrainian Catholic Church. This title made him the leader of Ukrainian Catholics throughout the world.

When the Germans invaded western Ukraine, Sheptytsky strongly opposed their Nazi rule. In 1942, he protested directly to one of Hitler's underlings about the destruction of the Jewish community in Ukraine. He also told the Pope in Rome about the Nazis' actions.

At Sheptytsky's urging, Christians in Ukraine saved the lives of thousands of Jews. Nuns and priests in Lviv hid about 200 Jewish children in convents, monasteries, and orphanages throughout the Lviv region. Some of these children even lived in Sheptytsky's home.

Sheptytsky died in 1944. His remains lie in a crypt in the Cathedral of Saint George in Lviv. In 1958, the Catholic Church in Rome started the procedure that might one day recognize Sheptytsky as a saint. Many Jews are also working to have Israel recognize him as a Righteous Gentile—the term used for non-Jews who saved Jews during World War II.

The Orthodox Calendar and Holy Days

Most Christians around the world celebrate Christmas on December 25, but the Ukrainian Orthodox Church follows a different calendar and celebrates Christmas on January 7. The church uses the Julian calender, which has thirteen more days than the Gregorian calendar. The Ukrainian Catholic Church also uses the Julian calendar. In 1582, Pope Gregory XIII adopted a new calendar for all Catholic countries. Orthodox countries, including Ukraine and Russia, stayed with the old calendar. All Orthodox holy days fall thirteen days after the same occasion in the rest of the world.

The most important holy days for Ukrainian Orthodox and Ukrainian Catholics are Easter and Christmas. During Lent, the forty days before Easter, Ukrainians prepare themselves

Important Religious Holidays

Christmas	January 7
Easter	March or April
St. Nicholas Day	December 6

Families wait outside a cathedral in Kyiv for the blessing of food at Easter.

spiritually and cleanse their homes. They purify their bodies by not eating meat or dairy products. They scrub their houses inside and out. The week before Easter, they prepare food for the Easter feast. Early on Easter morning, each family brings a basket filled with food to church. The priest blesses the food with holy water. This will be the first food eaten after a strict forty-day fast. Ukrainians enjoy their Easter foods, including the special Easter bread called *Paska*.

Children in costumes go caroling at Christmas.

During Christmas time in Ukraine, children go carol- ing. This is called *koliada*; the carolers are *koliadnyky*. The *koliadnyky* wear costumes much as children in the United States do for Halloween. The *koliadnyky* sing a song or recite a poem at each house. They are rewarded with candy or

money. On Christmas Eve, Ukrainian families get together for a meatless dinner that is called *sviata vecheria* (Blessed Supper). On Christmas Day, Ukrainians attend and celebrate the Liturgy. Gifts are not exchanged at Christmas in Ukraine. Gift giving takes place on St. Nicholas Day, which is December 6 on the Gregorian Calendar and December 19 on the Julian Calendar.

Churches, Monasteries, and Mosques

Ukraine's first churches were made of wood. Builders fitted logs together without using nails or glue. The logs were then covered by wooden shingles. Some wooden churches reached great heights with up to nine roof levels. The churches were capped with wooden-shingled cupolas or onion domes. Wooden bell towers were built separate from the churches so church roofs would not collapse under the bells' weight. Ukraine's oldest wooden churches have survived from the sixteenth century. Most of them stand in villages in the Carpathian Mountains. A good example of Ukrainian wooden churches is Saint Nicholas Church in the Museum of Folk Architecture and Folkways outside of Lviv. It was built in the 1700s. New churches in villages and small towns continue to be built from wood.

A wooden church in the Museum of Folk Architecture and Folkways in Lviv

Cathedral of Saint Sophia

Built between 1017 and 1037 under Yaroslav the Wise, the Cathedral of Saint Sophia is the oldest church today in Kyiv. For 900 years, the cathedral was the center of Ukrainian religious, political, and cultural life. It was the seat of the metropolitan of Ukraine's Orthodox Church. Kyivan princes were crowned, received ambassadors from other lands, and signed treaties in the cathedral. Kyiv's first library and school were also located in the cathedral. The cathedral's interior showed off the talents of eleventh-century artists and artisans.

The design of Saint Sophia was based on the *Hagia Sophia* (Holy Wisdom) in Constantinople, the main church of the Byzantine Empire. Originally, Saint Sophia had thirteen golden cupolas. The center cupola represented Christ, and the other twelve cupolas stood for the twelve apostles. During the Mongolian invasions, the cathedral was badly damaged. For many years it was abandoned. During the eighteenth century, the cathedral was reconstructed in a style called the Kozak baroque. White plaster then covered the cathedral's outside walls and six more cupolas were added.

Inside, the cathedral looks much as it did in the eleventh century. More than 2,000 square feet (186 sq m) of mosaics still cover the walls and floors. Throughout the cathedral, 25 shades of gold and silver were used in addition to 177 other colors. Large frescoes—paintings on plaster—also cover the walls. Besides religious scenes, the frescoes include portraits of Yaroslav and his family, pictures of wild animals, and scenes of everyday life in Kyivan Rus.

Large churches and cathedrals in Ukraine's cities are made of brick and stone. Ukraine's large churches are famous for their golden cupolas. All Ukrainian Orthodox and Ukrainian Catholic churches are built in the form of a cross, with sections extending equally in four directions. The main parts of each church are the vestibule, or entryway; the sanctuary; and the nave. The priests celebrate the Liturgy in the sanctuary, and the worshipers stand in the nave. A large carved wooden screen called an *iconostasis* separates the nave from the sanctuary. Each iconostasis has several rows of icons, or religious paintings. The Orthodox say that icons are "written," not painted, because they bring to life the truths found in the Bible.

The Caves Monastery, Kyiv

Ukraine's first icons were written by Byzantine artists during the time of Volodymyr the Great. Some icons are thought to have healing or protective powers. One of Ukraine's most famous icons is the "Mother of God" in the Dormition Cathedral at the Pochayiv Monastery. Many people believe it saved the monastery from the Tatar attack of 1675.

Monasteries are communities in which monks or nuns live, work, and study. The Caves Monastery in Kyiv is Ukraine's oldest and largest one. In

1051, two monks founded the monastery in caves along the Dnipro River. With the support of the Kyivan Rus princes, the

A Tatar mosque

Caves Monastery became a center of Orthodox learning. A cathedral, churches, and other buildings were constructed above the caves. Many monks were buried in niches in the caves. Their mummified remains are now seen from behind glass walls.

Mosques are places of worship for Muslims, the followers of Islam. The Tatars in Krym have restored mosques that were destroyed when Russia annexed Krym in 1783. The Uzbek Khan Mosque is the oldest Islamic building in Krym. It was built in 1314 in what is now the town of Staryy Krym. The largest mosque in Krym is the Dzhuma-Dzhami. It was built in Yevpatoria in the 1550s and 1560s. Both of these mosques are again places of worship.

Traditional Culture, Modern Sports

CULTURE AND SPORTS ARE SO IMPORTANT IN UKRAINE that the government has a minister of culture and a minister of sports. With independence, Ukraine's rich cultural traditions are thriving once more. Ukrainian literature, music, art, and theater continue to grow. Folk arts that date back hundreds, even thousands, of years are now handed down openly from one generation to the next.

Opposite: **Young dancers in traditional embroidered costumes**

Folk Arts

Ukrainian folk arts are recognized throughout the world for their beauty and quality. Throughout Ukraine, museums exhibit Ukrainian embroidery, weaving, ceramics, wood-carving, and decorated Easter eggs. Designs and colors used in Ukrainian folk art vary from region to region. However, geometric shapes and symbols of plants and animals appear in most Ukrainian folk art. In special schools and institutes, students learn the skills and techniques of creating Ukrainian folk art from master craftspeople. One of the best-known schools is the Hutsul Technical Art Institute in the Carpathian Mountain town of Kosiv. These skills are also passed down in families from mothers to daughters and from fathers to sons.

Embroidery is Ukraine's most widely practiced folk art. Women in many families still stitch designs onto blouses, skirts, shirts, and aprons. Depending on the design, it may take several months to a year to complete the embroidery.

These clothes are worn as folk costumes on holy days and holidays. Women also embroider *rushnyky*, which are long narrow towels. Rushnyky have special purposes with almost a religious meaning. They are often draped over the top and sides of icons in Ukrainian homes. Other rushnyky line baskets filled with breads and foods that are blessed at church on special occasions.

Pysanky, beautifully decorated Easter eggs, are perhaps the best-known Ukrainian folk art. In Ukrainian, *pysanky* comes from the word that means "to write." A design is written on an egg using wax applied by a sharp point of a pen. Then the hollowed out egg is dipped into a colored dye. When the egg dries, more design is applied with the wax pencil, and the egg is dipped into another colored dye. This process continues until the artist has completed the egg. Some pysanky artists design 500 to 600 eggs a year, but no two pysanky are alike. Pysanky have been made since pre-Christian times. Ancient Ukrainians believed pysanky would protect them from evil. At Easter, Ukrainians buy pysanky and have them blessed at church. They give them to family and friends as a wish for good health or as a sign of friendship.

Intricately designed *pysanky* (Easter eggs)

Weaving, ceramics, and wood-carving are other well-known Ukrainian crafts. The *kylym* is a heavy, brightly colored woven carpet. In Ukrainian homes, kylyms are not found on the floor. Instead, they are hung on the walls, where they provide insulation against the cold and wind. Since prehistoric times, people in Ukraine have made ceramic containers. High-quality clays still found throughout Ukraine make ceramics an important craft industry today. Modern Ukrainian potters make colorful vases, bowls, and other kinds of dishes. The Hutsuls are famous for their woodworking skills. They make decorative boxes and jar-like containers from fine woods. Inlaid in the wood are mother-of-pearl and various polished stones.

A *kylym* is the focal point of this small living room.

A collection of Ukrainian ceramics

In the 1700s, Hryhory Skovoroda and Ivan Kotlyarevsky wrote the first works using everyday spoken Ukrainian. Skovoroda aimed his poems at ordinary people. Kotlyarevsky's *Eneyida* retold the ancient tale of the Greek hero Ulysses by substituting Kozak heroes for the Greeks. That work also appealed to ordinary Ukrainians. Kotlyarevsky's best-known work is the novel *Natalka Poltavka*.

In the 1840s and 1850s, Taras Shevchenko wrote long poems in Ukrainian about Ukraine's history. He combined several Ukrainian dialects with Church Slavonic. The difference between earlier writers and Shevchenko could be compared to the difference between writing in American street slang and writing standard English. Yet Shevchenko wrote for the common people and was widely read by them. Shevchenko's works led the way for others to write in Ukrainian. Their poetry and novels told of village life in Ukraine and the injustices suffered by Ukraine's peasants.

Taras Shevchenko

During the same time that Shevchenko was writing poems in Ukrainian, Nikolai Gogol wrote plays and novels in Russian. *Taras Bulba*, a story about Kozak heroes, was made into a Hollywood movie in 1962. Gogol's play *The Inspector General* made fun of Russian government officials. Gogol, who was born near Poltava, wrote mainly for Russian readers. Ukrainians honor Gogol today with a monument and the Gogol Music and Drama Theater, both in Poltava. In Ukrainian, Gogol's name is pronounced *Hohol*.

Besides Shevchenko, Ukraine's most honored writers are Ivan Franko and Larisa Kosach-Kvitka. They wrote in the late

From Serf to Cultural Hero

Taras Shevchenko is Ukraine's most beloved poet. Schools, universities, and museums are named for him. Statues of him stand in parks and squares in towns and villages throughout Ukraine. Usually pictured with a bushy, Kozak-style moustache and wearing his curly, wool astrakhan hat, Shevchenko is even on Ukraine's money.

Shevchenko was born a serf in 1814 in the village of Moryntsi. As a young boy, he drew pictures on walls with lumps of coal. He copied paintings that hung in the landowner Pavel Engelhardt's home. In 1830, Engelhardt moved his household to Saint Petersburg, Russia, and took Shevchenko with him. There, Shevchenko met students from the Saint Petersburg Academy of Art. They saw Shevchenko's drawings and recognized his talents. In 1838, the students raised enough money to buy Shevchenko's freedom from Engelhardt.

With his freedom gained, Shevchenko began writing poetry. He published his first book of poems, *Kobzar* ("The Bard"), in 1840. Shevchenko's poems described Ukraine's land, its greatness under the Kozaks, the evils of serfdom, and the need for Ukraine to be free of Russian control. Some of his poems even foretold of a revolution in which Ukraine gained its freedom.

During the 1840s, Shevchenko joined the Brotherhood of Saints Cyril and Methodius. This group met in secret and aimed to overthrow the Russian tsar and abolish serfdom. Because of his membership in this group and the ideas in his poems, Tsar Nicholas I had Shevchenko arrested in 1847 and exiled to a military outpost near Kazakhstan. He was forbidden to write or paint, but the officers on the post had him tutor their children and paint portraits of their families. Shevchenko also continued to write poetry.

In 1857, two years after Nicholas I died, Tsar Alexander II released Shevchenko from exile and let him return to Saint Petersburg. In 1859, Shevchenko visited Ukraine but was arrested there for speaking out on his views and brought back to Saint Petersburg. He was forbidden to ever return to Ukraine. After Shevchenko died in 1861, his body was returned to Ukraine, where it was buried in Kaniv on a hill overlooking the Dnipro River. Today, visitors to Kaniv seek out the Shevchenko Museum to learn more about this great poet and patriot.

1800s and early 1900s. Franko wrote poetry, plays, short stories, and political essays. Kosach-Kvitka loved Ukraine so much that she wrote poems and plays under the pen name Lesia Ukrainka. Her poems expressed beauty, hope, and strength. Both Franko and Ukrainka became involved with political groups that opposed tsarist control of Ukraine and supported independence. Because of their political thoughts,

Franko and Ukrainka were arrested and imprisoned for short periods of time. Today, Ukrainka is still regarded as Ukraine's most important female poet; statues of her stand in many Ukrainian cities. Franko has been especially honored in Lviv, where he spent his last years. A park in the center of Lviv was named for him, and the Franko Literary-Memorial Museum has exhibits of his manuscripts, letters, and books.

During the Soviet era, many Ukrainian writers were killed or imprisoned. Those who were left had to write in the style known as Socialist Realism. Stories done in this style praised the Soviet workers and the programs of the Soviet government. Heroes in these stories had to be perfect; they couldn't have problems or conflicts in values.

For a brief time in the 1960s, writers in the Soviet Union were allowed more freedom. Ukrainians who used this new freedom were called Writers of the Sixties. Leading writers of that group were Lina Kostenko and Vasyl Stus. Through her book of poems, *Journey of the Heart*, Kostenko gained worldwide fame. Stus's best-known poetry is *Winter Trees* and *Candle in the Mirror*. The poems express the pain felt by writers who are not allowed to tell the truth. In the 1970s, the Soviets again clamped down on freedom of expression and silenced the Writers of the Sixties. Stus and other writers died in Soviet prisons and labor camps.

During *glasnost*, in the 1980s, members of the Ukrainian Writers' Union published works that helped convince Ukrainians to seek independence. Since its independence, the creativity of Ukraine's writers has been reborn. For example,

Ihor Kalynets uses free verse in his poems that deal with issues facing Ukraine today.

Theater and Film

In 1881, the tsar's government allowed plays to be performed in the Ukrainian language. That same year, in Kirovohrad, Marko Kropyvnytsky founded Ukraine's first professional theater. By the 1930s, most Ukrainian cities had theaters. Today, Ukraine's sixty-some theaters produce plays by Ivan Franko, Lesia Ukrainka, and modern Ukrainian writers. Plays translated into Ukrainian from Russian, English, and other languages are also produced. Mykola Khvylovy's *Me*, written in 1924, is a popular Ukrainian production. It presents the struggle between political loyalty and duty to family.

Ukrainian directors have been making films since the 1890s. Early short films were filmed outdoors. Ukraine's first film studios opened in Kyiv and Odesa in 1915. In the 1920s, Oleksander Dovzhenko gained worldwide fame directing silent films. His *Zvenyhora*, *Arsenal*, and *The Earth* dealt with the effects of the Russian Revolution on Ukraine. Dovzhenko's films are regarded as some of the world's best silent-movies. In 1964, director Serhiy Paradzhanov's *Shadows of Forgotten Ancestors* won praise from Western critics. Based on a novel by nineteenth-century writer Mykhailo Kotsyubynsky, the film tells a story of love, death, and revenge in a Hutsul village in the Carpathians. Today, young Ukrainian directors show their work to a world audience at the International Film Festival held in Kyiv each October.

Playing the bandura

Ukrainians enjoy folk, classical, and popular music. Ukrainian folk instruments include stringed instruments such as the *tsymbaly* and the *bandura*. The tsymbaly is played somewhat like a xylophone. The bandura is Ukraine's national instrument. It has between forty-five and sixty strings that are plucked like harp strings. During the Kozak period and nineteenth century, only blind men called *kobzars* played the bandura. As they played, the kobzars recited long poems, called *dumy*. The dumy told about Ukraine's Kozak history and how the Ukrainian people struggled against invaders. Today, women also play the bandura. The instrument is used now to accompany folk dancers and has an important part in orchestras.

Famous Opera Houses

The opera and ballet theaters in Odesa and Lviv look much like Austria's famous Vienna State Opera House. Odesa's opera house was designed by Austrian architects and was built from 1884 to 1887. Busts of Ukrainian and Russian writers, including Gogol, decorate the outside of the building. Inside, opera fans can sit in 1 of 1,560 seats in five tiers. Once seated, they can look up at the ceiling and enjoy scenes from the plays of William Shakespeare.

The Lviv Opera and Ballet Theatre was designed by Zygmunt Gorgolewsky and built between 1897 and 1900. Three huge sculptures on top of the building represent Love, Glory, and Victory. Recently, the building was renamed the Ivan Franko Opera and Ballet Theatre.

Other folk instruments are the flutelike *sopilka* and the *trembita*, a hollowed-out birch tree trunk 10 feet (3 m) long. Hutsuls play the trembita in high pastures in the Carpathian Mountains. The instrument's sad, muffled sound once sent messages between mountain villages. Today, Hutsuls play trembitas at funerals and folk festivals.

One of Ukraine's best-known classical musicians and composers was Mykola Lysenko. He is called the Father of Ukrainian National Music. Lysenko wrote operas and symphonies in the late 1800s. Many of his operas, such as *Taras Bulba* and *Natalka from Poltava*, were based on works by Ukrainian writers. Lysenko also studied Ukrainian folk songs. He wove their rhythms and melodies into his works for symphony orchestras. In the early 1900s, Mykola Leontovych wrote music for choral groups. His best-known work throughout the world is "*Shchedryk*" ("Epiphany Carol"). In English, this song is called "The Carol of the Bells" and is heard at Christmas. Today, Myroslav Skoryk is a leading composer of symphonies and film scores. He is best known for *Carpathian Rhapsody* and the film score for *Shadows of Forgotten Ancestors*.

Ukrainians also enjoy popular music such as jazz, rock, and heavy metal. Volodymyr Ivasyuk blended Ukrainian folk music with popular music. Before he was found hanged in Chernivtsi in 1979, he wrote more than fifty songs. Because the Soviet government frequently hounded him, many people believe the Soviet secret police killed him. His best-known song, "*Chervona Ruta*" ("Red Rue Blossom"), has become the name of the music festival held every two years since 1989 in Ukraine. Today, other popular singers and rock groups perform in clubs in Ukraine's cities. There's even a website where fans can listen to the top tunes of the week and vote for their favorite.

Folk Dance and Ballet

Folk dances have been popular in Ukraine since ancient times. The first dances celebrated the change in seasons and special occasions, such as birth, marriage, and death. Later, in early Christian times, young girls performed circle dances, called *hahilky*, at Easter. The most famous Ukrainian folk dance is the Kozak dance known as the *hopak*. In this dance,

Red-booted folk dancers perform in Kyiv.

Veseli Cherevychky ("Jolly Boots")

In 1990, the Folk Children Dance Ballet known as *Veseli Cherevychky* (Jolly Boots) was formed in Lviv. Children from ages four to fourteen take part in Jolly Boots. They sing, dance, and act during their programs. The group's purpose is to acquaint Ukrainians with their country's traditional songs and dances and to share Ukrainian culture with other people throughout the world. Jolly Boots has performed at EuroDisney in France and at festivals in Poland, Germany, and the United States. The children begin and end each program with these words: "We sincerely love our land, we love Ukraine."

the performers squat down low and kick out their feet and then jump into the air. The movements of the hopak started as exercises to prepare Kozaks for battle. Today, professional folk dance troupes perform many of these same dances on stages in Ukraine and in other countries.

Ballets were first performed in Ukraine in the 1700s. However, the first ballets written by Ukrainians weren't staged until the 1930s. Later, during the Soviet era, Russian ballets took the spotlight. However, during the thaw in the 1950s, ballets based on poems by Taras Shevchenko and Lesia Ukrainka were written and performed. Since *glasnost* and independence, Ukrainian composers have produced more than fifty ballets. They are performed at ballet theaters in Kyiv, Lviv, Odesa, Kharkiv, Dnipropetrovsk, and Donetsk.

Art

By the 1700s and 1800s, many Ukrainian artists studied at the Saint Petersburg Academy of Arts and worked on paintings in Saint Petersburg, Russia. As a result, they are sometimes misidentified as Russian artists. Some of these artists were sculptor Ivan Martos and portrait painters Dmytro Levytsky

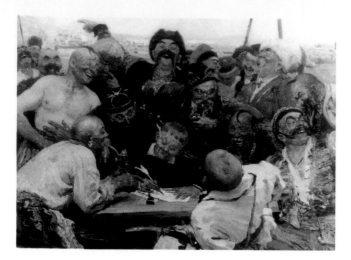

Kozaks Writing a Letter to the Turkish Sultan by Ilya Repin

and Volodymyr Borovykovsky. Taras Shevchenko and Ilya Repin are two better-known artists from the 1800s. Shevchenko painted more than 1,000 works, including portraits and scenes of life in the Ukrainian countryside. Repin is known for his historical paintings of Kozaks and his portraits of famous writers such as Leo Tolstoy, Gogol, and Maxim Gorky. Arkhip Kuindzhi painted landscapes of the Ukrainian steppes and the Dnipro River.

During the Soviet era, Socialist Realism also ruled in painting and sculpture. Since its independence, Ukrainian artists have blossomed in their new freedom. Their main theme is to show the truth of life. Some present this theme by painting traditional country villages, Kozaks, and bandura players from the past. Others, such as sculptor Yevhen Prokopov and painter Volodymyr Podlevsky, have done modern religious pieces. One of Podlevsky's pieces shows an angel giving energy to earth. Oleksander Dubovyk is known for his abstract paintings. Many of them show struggle; others, unity. Dubovyk also created colorful stained glass windows for new churches in Kyiv. Both Prokopov and Dubovyk have held exhibits in the United States.

Sports

During the Soviet era, Ukraine's athletes played on the Soviet Union's teams and helped them win world championships and Olympic gold medals. Today, Ukraine's athletes compete as

Ukrainians for Ukraine. Ordinary Ukrainians of all ages take part in sports for recreation and fitness. They enjoy playing tennis, hiking, bicycling, taking aerobics and yoga classes, and participating in other individual and team sports.

Soccer, also called association football, is the national sport of Ukraine. Ukraine's first official soccer match was held in 1894. Today, Ukraine has sixteen professional soccer teams from fifteen cities. Kyiv has two teams. Dynamo Kyiv is Ukraine's best-known team because it has won many USSR and European championships. Dynamo Kyiv has also taken part in World Cup games. Besides watching the pros play, thousands of Ukrainian children and adults also play soccer. They are members of local soccer clubs.

Since its independence, some Ukrainian athletes have left Ukraine to play on U.S. or European teams. Andrei Shevchenko, a Dynamo Kyiv star, plays in Milan, Italy.

The Deadly Soccer Game

During World War II, Germany occupied Ukraine, including Kyiv. Because of wartime conditions, regular soccer games were no longer played. According to many reports, the Dynamo Kyiv soccer team worked in a bakery and practiced soccer in an empty lot. In the summer of 1942, German officials organized a "friendly" game between Dynamo Kyiv and a team from the German army. The German team had never lost a game. On June 14, Kyivan citizens and German government officials and army officers filled the stadium. Instead of losing the game as they had been told to, the Dynamo team was leading 4 to 1 in the second half. The referee ended the game before the time was up and before the Germans could officially lose the game.

The angry Germans then arranged matches for Dynamo against even stronger German teams. Dynamo continued to win. Finally on August 9, Dynamo met the powerful German Flakelf team and beat them, too. After that game, the Germans arrested four Dynamo players and executed them at Babyn Yar. Today, a large sculpture honoring the executed players stands in front of Dynamo Stadium in Kyiv.

Alexander Volkov, now Ukraine's minister of sports, was once a professional basketball player with the Atlanta Hawks. Vitaly Potapenko, called the "Ukrainian Train," is a center for the Boston Celtics. Dmitri Khristich has played forward for National

Boston Celtic Vitaly Potapenko

Hockey League teams in the United States. Figure skater Oksana Baiul, who in 1994 won independent Ukraine's first Olympic gold medal, now lives and skates in the United States.

Many athletes, however, continue to play in Ukraine and represent it in the Olympics and other world championships. Serhiy Bubka set the men's world pole vault record of 6.14 meters (20 ft) in 1994. Inessa Kravets set the women's world triple jump record of 15.5 meters (50.9 ft) in 1995. Andrei Medvedev and Elena Tatarkova compete on tennis courts in international championships. Ukrainian boxers Eduard Lutsker and Serhiy Kostenko have also done well in worldwide competitions.

Oksana Baiul performs at the 1994 Olympics.

Lilia Podkopayeva—Ukraine's First Olympic Double Gold Medalist

In 1996, Ukraine's team at the Olympic Games in Atlanta, Georgia, won nine gold medals. Seventeen-year-old gymnast Lilia Podkopayeva from Donetsk won two of them. She became Ukraine's first Olympic multimedal winner. She not only took home a gold medal for best floor exercise but also won the gold for individual all-around champion, which includes the vault, uneven bars, and balance beam routines. With that gold medal, Podkopayeva became the first woman to hold World, European, and Olympic championships in the all-around.

Since the 1996 Olympic Games, Podkopayeva coaches at summer gymnastic training camps in the United States. In the fall, she returns to Ukraine and continues her own training.

Daily Life and Special Occasions

Even though Ukraine's economy is struggling, daily life for most Ukrainians goes on much as it has since before independence. Adults go to work; young adults pursue studies at universities or institutes; and children attend school. Men and women spend much time in lines to purchase food, but generally there is food to buy. Ukrainians also have fun. They enjoy getting together in their homes with family and friends for casual dinners. At other times, Ukrainian families rejoice over births, christenings, and marriages, or to honor the dead.

Opposite: **A Ukrainian family at home**

Ukrainian Marriage Customs

From birth to death, Ukrainians observe special customs that mark a person's passage through life. Ukraine's regions, villages, and families each has its own customs and traditions. Many customs surround Ukrainian weddings, which can last three or more days. Over the three days, the bride and groom first sign the civil marriage contract, which shows that the government recognizes the marriage. Then they take part in a church ceremony. After the official ceremonies are over, they are honored at many celebrations. One of the most famous Ukrainian wedding customs centers on the *korovai*, a round loaf of bread decorated with doves and topped by tree branches—all made from dough. The korovai symbolizes long life and many children. The bride's family makes the korovai. When the groom comes to the

bride's house, the bride's parents say a special blessing over the kneeling couple and present them with the korovai. In some villages, the bride and groom cut the korovai and share it with their wedding guests. In other villages, the couple saves the korovai because it is so beautiful and took so much time to make.

Celebrating age-old holidays and festivals provides breaks in the daily routine throughout the year.

Daily Meals and Special Foods

As in most countries, food plays an important part in Ukrainians' daily lives, as well as in their holidays and festivals. Meals are prepared carefully, and the table setting is arranged with great thought. A Ukrainian family's breakfast might include a bowl of *kasha* (hot cereal), wheat or rye *khlib* (bread), fried or scrambled eggs, and farmer's *syr* (cheese), which is similar to cottage cheese. *Moloko* (milk), *chai* (tea), *kava* (coffee) with moloko, and fruit juice are also part of a Ukrainian breakfast. Sometimes Ukrainians make a breakfast sandwich of khlib, *kovbasa* (sausage), and syr. Ukrainians eat a hearty breakfast because their next meal, dinner, is not served until late afternoon.

Dinner starts out with a soup—borsch or chicken noodle soup. A salad such as one made of sour cabbage, tomatoes,

Borsch is a hearty soup made of beets.

cucumbers, peppers, and onion is also served. The main dish might be pork, chicken, or turkey, with potatoes, noodles, or macaroni. A dessert of plums, apples, or cookies ends the meal. Pies, cakes, and other rich desserts are saved for special occasions. Supper is a light meal eaten in the early evening. It might be soup, sliced bread with jam, a cheese and sausage sandwich, or maybe leftovers from dinner.

The foods for which Ukraine is famous are usually served on Sundays and special occasions. *Varenyky* are stuffed dumplings made from a soft rolled dough and filled with ground meat, potatoes, cheese, or sauerkraut. Dessert varenyky are filled with cherries, blueberries, or other fruits. *Holubtsi* are cabbage rolls stuffed with ground meat and rice. *Kotleta po Kyivsky*, better known as Chicken Kiev, was first made sometime during the period of Soviet control of Ukraine. This butter-stuffed and breaded, boneless chicken breast was first served to impress Soviet government officials.

Bread, of course, is an important part of all Ukrainian meals. Because each region of the country has its own breads, there are hundreds of different kinds. Special breads are also made for various occasions. For example, *kolach* is a braided bread formed into three rings. It is served on Christmas Eve.

Borsch—Ukraine's National Dish

Borsch is beet soup. There are almost as many borsch recipes as there are regions in Ukraine. Borsch can include a variety of vegetables, may contain meat, and can be served hot or cold. However, borsch is always served with a dollop of sour cream. A recipe for simple borsch is given here. Ukrainian cooks might add chopped carrots, potatoes, and other vegetables, as well as chunks of beef, lamb, or pork to this recipe.

3 quarts (2.8 l) water
3 pounds (1.36 kg) peeled and cut beets
1 cup (227 g) chopped celery
1 sliced onion
1/8 teaspoon (1.75 g) salt
2 tablespoons (28.35 g) chopped dill
1/4 cup (59 ml) sour cream
1 tablespoon (15 ml) lemon juice

Bring water to a boil. Place beets, celery, and onion in the boiling water. Cover, and turn down heat. Simmer for 30 to 40 minutes. Add salt. Sprinkle dill on borsch. Ladle borsch into soup bowls. Place a large spoonful of sour cream in the middle of each bowl of borsch. Serves eight to nine people.

Country Houses and City Apartments

In both the country and the city, the kitchen is the most important room in the Ukrainian home. That is where meals are prepared and eaten. In many rural homes, the ceramic oven in the kitchen is not only used for cooking but also provides heat for the rest of the house.

People who reside in villages in Ukraine own their homes. Many homes in the country are white-washed, one-story buildings with colorful decorations. They have a kitchen, a living room and a bedroom. At night, the living room becomes another bedroom if needed. Few village houses have indoor plumbing. Families draw water from a well for cooking and bathing. The toilet is in an outbuilding in the backyard. Also in the yard are a vegetable garden and, possibly, an outbuilding to shelter a cow and chickens. Village families raise much of their own food. Any surplus vegetables or eggs are taken to nearby city markets and sold or traded for other goods.

In the cities, Ukrainians live in apartments. Since independence, some Ukrainians have purchased their apartment from the government. Others still pay rent to the government. Depending on the size of the apartment, rents run U.S.$15 to U.S.$40 a month and include utilities. Owners of privatized apartments pay about U.S.$15 to U.S.$40 a month for utilities and building maintenance. Average wages are only U.S.$25 to U.S.$40 a month, however,

A kitchen in a Kyiv apartment

and by law, families cannot spend more than 15 percent of their income for rent or utilities. The government pays for anything over 15 percent.

The average apartment has a kitchen, a bathroom, and from one to three other rooms. The toilet and the bathtub are sometimes in separate rooms. Because people continue to move from villages to the cities, a housing shortage has developed. For example, a three-room apartment might be home to five or six people—one or two children, their parents, and one set of grandparents. In such an apartment, there is a living room and two bedrooms—one for the grandparents and the other for the parents. At night, the living room becomes a bedroom for the children.

Although apartment dwellers have electricity and indoor plumbing, these utilities sometimes operate unevenly. Electrical outages occur frequently. In some cities, electric power rotates from section to section throughout the day, as in a "rolling blackout" in the United States. Water service is another problem. Sometimes the water is rusty and undrinkable. Other times there is no water, or no hot water. Ukrainians do the best they can under such conditions. They draw extra water when it is on so they will have enough when the water is off. For washing and bathing, they heat small amounts of water to warm up the cold water.

Ukrainian Hospitality

In spite of home-related inconveniences, Ukrainians love to gather family and friends in their homes for food and conversation. Ukrainians are generous hosts. In fact, there's a saying that you can't out-give a Ukrainian. They make sure that their guests eat the best and the most food at every meal. If a guest is staying for a few days, the Ukrainian family gives up its best bed for the guest.

At one time, Ukrainian hosts greeted their guests at the door with a loaf of bread resting on a rushnyky and topped with a mound of salt. From this gesture, guests knew that they were welcome and that they could share all that the host had. This custom is now observed only on special occasions, such as when the Ukrainian government welcomes an official from another country.

Going to School

Ukrainian children spend a good part of their life in school. The school year runs from September 1 to May 25 and has four quarters. Before summer vacation begins, students return for two weeks of exams in June. Between quarters, students enjoy breaks of from one to two weeks. In Ukraine, secondary school covers what are grades four through eleven in the United States. In grades five through eight, students attend five to seven classes each day. Classes run for forty-five minutes, and there are breaks of ten to twenty minutes between classes.

In the course of a week, middle-school students (grades 5–8) have classes in the Ukrainian language, Ukrainian literature, a foreign language, world literature, Ukrainian history, world history, geography, algebra, geometry, biology, chemistry, physics, physical education, music, and art. At some schools,

Art school children prepare for a concert.

students also take environment and civics classes. Students attend each class only once or twice a week, however. Part of the school day is also spent in activities such as chess and karate, putting on plays, learning folktales and folk songs, and choir and band. After school, students might have additional music lessons or play soccer, hockey, or tennis.

Games Children Play

Children in Ukraine enjoy playing games outdoors with friends at school or in their neighborhoods after school. One game that girls play is called *resynochki*, or rubber bands. In this game, two girls face each other, standing about an arm's length apart. They place a long thick elastic band around the backs of their ankles. Other girls then take turns jumping with different movements over and through the rubber band.

First a girl jumps and lands with both legs inside the rubber band; then she jumps and lands with one leg between the band and one leg on the outside of the band; finally she jumps and lands with one leg outside the band and the other leg inside the rubber band. Then the two girls move the rubber band up higher on their legs and the same girl tries to do the jumps again. If she fails to do the jumps at the new height, she's out, and another girl gets a turn. If she succeeds, the rubber band is moved higher still. The band can be moved as high as the two girls' waists.

Lviv State University students socialize in a dorm room.

When students finish secondary school, they may continue their education at a technical or vocational school or at a university. Since all of these schools are located in cities, students in Ukrainian villages must leave home. Ukrainian universities and technical and vocational schools do not have campuses. The main classroom building is usually near the downtown area. Other classroom buildings are found throughout the city, and dormitories are located in other neighborhoods.

Time to Relax

At least 10 percent of Ukraine's city dwellers own a *dacha*, a cottage in the country. As often as they can, Ukrainians spend

A country *dacha* and garden

a day off or a weekend at the dacha. It provides a break from the work, noise, and sometimes dirty air of the cities. In the yard around the dacha, families plant fruits and vegetables. Gardens can include apricot and apple trees, grapevines, strawberry and raspberry plants, potatoes, tomatoes, cucumbers, carrots, and onions. On visits to the dacha, owners cultivate their gardens and harvest ripe fruits and vegetables to bring them back to the city. In this way, they supplement their diets with fresh foods that are not always available in the city markets. Many families also pickle or preserve these fruits and vegetables so they can enjoy them in the winter.

In Ukraine, workers receive three or four weeks of vacation each year. Most of them take their vacations in the summer. If they don't have a dacha, many visit family members who live in villages throughout Ukraine. Some Ukrainians vacation at Black Sea resorts near Odesa or along the Krymian coast. During the Soviet era, the beach area of Krym was called the Russian Riviera. Russian government officials and Communist Party leaders vacationed there. Ukraine's mountains also attract vacationers.

National Holidays in Ukraine	
New Year's Day	January 1
International Women's Day	March 8
Victory Day (1945)	May 9
Independence Day	August 24
Liberation Day (1944)	October 28

Festivals and National Holidays

Sviato is the Ukrainian word for festival. Beginning with New Year's Day on January 1, Ukraine's calendar is marked with many a sviato. A few days before New Year's Day, families decorate a pine tree in their homes. On New Year's Eve, people gather at homes for parties. At midnight, fireworks are set off

In downtown Kyiv a World War II veteran dances during Victory Day celebrations.

outside and everyone greets the new year. Many Ukrainians stay up all night, singing, dancing, eating, and drinking.

Several festivals and holidays take place each spring. International Women's Day falls on March 8. This national holiday started during the Soviet era as a way to mark the struggle for women's equality. Now, on International Women's Day Ukrainian men and boys honor their mothers, wives, and sisters with cards, flowers, and maybe a special dinner. Victory Day, on May 9, is another Ukrainian national holiday. This holiday marks the end of World War II in Europe and honors the 7.5 million Ukrainians who died during that war. Each village and city in Ukraine has a monument to the war dead.

The Harvest Festival is celebrated each autumn. This celebration started thousands of years ago. Early Ukrainians thanked the gods for a good harvest. Today, in the main cities of regions throughout Ukraine, farmers display their best crops and livestock. Prizes are awarded to the best exhibits. Children take part in athletic contests, and folk singers and dancers perform in traditional costumes.

Traditional Dress

The patterns and colors of Ukrainian traditional dress vary from region to region. However, there are many basic similarities among all regions. Women's headdresses are woven with flowers and have colorful streamers that flow down their backs. Women also wear heavily embroidered white blouses. An embroidered vest is worn over the blouse. They also wear a colorful embroidered wool skirt over a white petticoat that peeks out from under the skirt. High red leather boots complete the outfit.

Men wear white shirts with less embroidery than on the women's blouses. They wear a vest or a long coat over the shirt. Men's pants are baggy-legged and tied at the waist with a sash and at the ankles with laces. The loose clothing makes it easy for them to dance. Red leather boots are also part of Ukrainian traditional dress for men. Today, traditional clothing is worn only for festivals, holidays, and special occasions such as Christmas and weddings. Folksingers and traditional dancers also wear these clothes when performing.

Ukraine's newest holiday is Independence Day, August 24. On that day in 1991, Ukraine declared independence from the Soviet Union. Ukrainians celebrate Independence Day with parades, fireworks, folk songs, concerts and festivals, and many traditional foods.

Timeline

Ukrainian History

People are living in Ukraine.	**Ca. 148,000** B.C.
Trypillians are farming in Ukraine.	**Ca. 5000– 2000** B.C.
Cimmerians, Scythians, Sarmatians, Goths, and Huns each control the steppe for long periods of time.	**1500** B.C.– A.D. **375**
Historians record the founding of Kyiv.	**Late 400s**
East Slavs have moved into Ukraine.	**600s**
Rus leader Oleh becomes the first Kyivan prince.	**882**
Princess Olha, ruler of Kyivan Rus, converts to Byzantine Christianity.	**957**
Volodymyr the Great makes Byzantine Christianity the official religion of Kyivan Rus.	**988**
Yaroslav the Wise expands Kyivan Rus territory to its greatest extent.	**1036–1054**
Kyiv falls to the Tatars.	**1240**
Principality of Galicia-Volhynia rises to power under prince Danylo and Prince Lev.	**1238–1301**
Galicia becomes part of the Kingdom of Poland; Volhynia becomes part of the Grand Duchy of Lithuania.	**1380**
Kozaks build a fort that becomes the Zaporizhzhyan Sich.	**1553–1554**
Volhynia comes under Poland's rule.	**1569**
The Union of Brest creates the Ukrainian Uniate Church.	**1596**
Bohdan Khmelnytsky leads the Kozaks against Poland.	**1648**
Khmelnytsky makes an alliance with Tsar Peter I of Russia.	**1654**

World History

2500 B.C.	Egyptians build the Pyramids and Sphinx in Giza.
563 B.C.	Buddha is born in India.
A.D. **313**	The Roman emperor Constantine recognizes Christianity.
610	The prophet Muhammad begins preaching a new religion called Islam.
1054	The Eastern (Orthodox) and Western (Roman) Churches break apart.
1066	William the Conqueror defeats the English in the Battle of Hastings.
1095	Pope Urban II proclaims the First Crusade.
1215	King John seals the Magna Carta.
1300s	The Renaissance begins in Italy.
1347	The Black Death sweeps through Europe.
1453	Ottoman Turks capture Constantinople, conquering the Byzantine Empire.
1492	Columbus arrives in North America.
1500s	The Reformation leads to the birth of Protestantism.

Ukrainian History

Russia and Poland divide Ukraine between them.	1667
At the Battle of Poltava, the Kozaks meet defeat by the tsar's army.	1709
In western Ukraine, Austria gains Galicia.	1772
Russia gains Poland's Ukrainian land west of the Dnipro and Volhynia.	1793–1795
Peasants in Russian-held Ukraine are serfs.	1783–1861
Four governments proclaim an independent Ukrainian National Republic.	1918–1921
Eastern Ukraine becomes the Ukrainian Soviet Socialist Republic; Poland regains Galicia and Volhynia; the Ukrainian Autocephalous Orthodox Church is founded.	1921
Soviet Ukraine becomes part of the USSR.	1922
Soviet leader Joseph Stalin begins collectivizing Ukraine's farms.	1929
About 7 million Ukrainian peasants die from starvation.	1932–1933
Ukraine becomes a battleground between German and Soviet armies.	1939–1945
Soviet leader Mikhail Gorbachev begins programs for economic reform and openness.	1954
Explosion occurs at the Chornobyl nuclear power plant.	1986
The People's Front of Ukraine for Reconstruction (RUKH) is formed.	1989
RUKH works for independence.	1990
Ukraine declares independence from Soviet Union; Ukrainians elect their first president.	1991
Ukraine joins the Organization for Security and Cooperation in Europe.	1992
Leonid Kuchma is elected president; Ukraine joins NATO's Partnership for Peace program.	1993
Ukraine's legislature adopts the nation's first constitution.	1996
Ukraine sends troops to join NATO peace-keeping forces in Kosovo; Kuchma is reelected.	1999
Ukraine wins 23 medals at the Olympic Games in Sydney, Australia—3 gold, 10 silver, and 10 bronze; the Chornobyl nuclear power plant is officially closed.	2000

World History

1776	The Declaration of Independence is signed.
1789	The French Revolution begins.
1865	The American Civil War ends.
1914	World War I breaks out.
1917	The Bolshevik Revolution brings Communism to Russia.
1929	Worldwide economic depression begins.
1939	World War II begins, following the German invasion of Poland.
1957	The Vietnam War starts.
1989	The Berlin Wall is torn down, as Communism crumbles in Eastern Europe.
1996	Bill Clinton is re-elected U.S. president.
2000	George W. Bush is elected U.S. president.

Fast Facts

Official name: Ukrayina (Ukraine)

Capital: Kyiv

Official language: Ukrainian

A village in the Carpathians

Ukraine's flag

Young dancers in costume

Official religion:	None
Year of founding:	1991
Founder:	The Ukrainian people
National anthem:	"Ukraine Lives On" (*Shche Ne Vmerla Ukrayina*); words by Pavlo Chubynsky, music by V. Verbytsky
Government:	Unitary, multiparty republic
Chief of state:	President
Head of government:	Prime minister
Area and dimensions:	233,090 square miles (603,656 sq km) Length east–west: 830 miles (1,336 km) Length north–south: 550 miles (885 km)
Latitude and longitude of geographic center:	49° North, 32° East
Land and water borders:	Russia to the east and northeast; Belarus to the north; Poland, Slovakia, and Hungary to the west; Romania and Moldava to the southwest; the Black Sea and the Sea of Azov to the south
Highest elevation:	Mount Hoverlya, 6,762 feet (2,061 m) above sea level
Lowest elevation:	Sea level along the Black Sea
Average temperature extremes:	In January, 18°F (36°C); in July, 77°F (25°C)
Average precipitation extremes:	From 11.7 inches (30 cm) in coastal lowlands along the Black Sea to 59 inches (150 cm) in the Carpathian Mountains
National population (1999 est.):	49,811,174

Saint George's Cathedral,
Lviv

**Population of largest
cities (1998):**

Kyiv	2,600,000
Dontsk	2,065,000
Kharkiv	1,521,000
Dnipropetrovsk	1,122,000
Odesa	1,027,000

Famous landmarks:
- ▶ *Caves Monastery*, Kyiv
- ▶ *Falz-Fein Askania-Nova Biosphere Reserve*, southeastern Ukraine
- ▶ *Ivan Franko Opera and Ballet Theatre*, Lviv
- ▶ *Museum of Folk Architecture and Folkways*, one near Kyiv and another outside of Lviv
- ▶ *Nikitsky Botanical Garden*, near Yalta
- ▶ *Odesa Opera and Ballet Theatre*
- ▶ *Saint George Cathedral*, Lviv
- ▶ *Saint Sophia Cathedral*, Kyiv
- ▶ *Sofiyyivka Arboretum and National Park*, in Uman

Industry: Ukraine's economy is slowly converting from producing goods for the military and heavy industry to making more consumer goods. More automobiles, refrigerators, television sets, washing machines, clothing, and shoes are available. However, iron and steel products continue to lead Ukraine's manufactured goods. Coal, iron ore, and manganese, Ukraine's leading mining products are used in the nation's steelmaking industry.

Currency: The hryvnia; in late 2000, U.S.$1 = 5.44 hryvnia

System of weights and measures: Metric system

Currency

Folk dancers perform in Kyiv.

Lilia Podkopayeva

Literacy rate (1995): 98.8 percent

Common Ukrainian words:

bandura (bahn-DOO-roo)	harp-like stringed instrument
chai (CHAH-yu)	tea
holubtsi (HO-loob-tsee)	stuffed cabbage rolls
kasha (KAH-shoo)	hot cereal
kava (KAH-voo)	coffee
khlib (khleeb)	bread
kotleta po Kyivsky (kot-LEH-tih pi KIH-yeev-s'kih)	chicken Kyiv
moloko (mo-lo-KAH)	milk
pysanky (PIH-sahn-kih)	decorated Easter eggs
syr (sihr)	farmer's cheese
varenyky (vah-REH-nih-kih)	stuffed dumplings

Famous people:

Ivan Franko (1856–1916)
Writer

Sergei Korolov (1906–1966)
Rocket engineer

Larisa Kosach-Kvitka (1871–1913)
(Lesia Ukrainka)
Poet

Leonid Kravchuk (1934–)
First democratically elected president

Lilia Podkopayeva (1978–)
Olympic gymnast

Andrei Sheptytsky (1865–1944)
Religious leader

Taras Shevchenko (1814–1861)
Poet and patriot

Volodymyr the Great (ruled 980–1015)
Kyivan prince

Yaroslav the Wise (ruled 1036–1054)
Kyivan prince

To Find Out More

Books

▶ Bassis, Vladimir. *Ukraine*. Festivals of the World. Milwaukee: Gareth Stevens Publishing, 1998.

▶ *Christmas in Ukraine*. Christmas around the World series. Chicago: World Book, 1997.

▶ Clay, Rebecca. *Ukraine: A New Independence*. Exploring Cultures of the World. New York: Benchmark Books, 1997.

▶ Farley, Marta Pisetska. *Festive Ukrainian Cooking*. Pittsburgh: University of Pittsburgh Press, 1990.

▶ Gray, Bettyanne. *Manya's Story: Faith and Survival in Revolutionary Russia* [Ukraine]. Minneapolis: Runestone Press, 1992. The story of Gray's mother's ordeals during programs in Russian Ukraine, 1917–1921.

▶ Hodge, Linda, and George Chumak. *Ukraine: Hippocrene Language and Travel Guide*. New York: Hippocrene Books, 1994.

▶ Oparenko, Christina. *Ukrainian Folk Tales*. Oxford, England: Oxford University Press, 1996.

▶ Otfinoski, Steven. *Ukraine*. Nations in Transition. New York: Facts on File, 1999.

▶ Osborn, Kevin. *The Ukrainian Americans*. The People of North America. New York: Chelsea House Publishers, 1989.

▶ *Ukrainian Heritage Dictionary*. Toronto: Editions Renyi, 1989.

Video Recordings

▶ Harencar, Oleg. *Ukraine: Ancient Crossroads, Modern Dreams*. San Ramon, Calif.: International Video Network, 1993.

▶ *Ukraine: The Land and Its People.* Toronto, Canada: Ukrainian Media Centre, 1992.

Websites

▶ **BRAMA-Gateway Ukraine— Arts and Culture**
http://brama.com/art/index.htm/
Links to artists, galleries, theaters, museums, literature, language, traditions, holidays, and folklore.

▶ **Center for Economic Initiative: Ukraine Regions**
http://www.ukrainebiz.com/Articles/ukraine_regions.htm
Information on geography, climate, population, and economy of each region of Ukraine.

▶ **InfoUkes**
http://www.infoukes.com
Provides information on history, technology, culture, religion, sports, in Ukraine, as well as links to other sites about Ukraine.

▶ **Ukrainian Top 10: The Best of Ukrainian Music**
http://music.uar.net/index_eng.html
Allows visitors to vote for their favorite popular song, listen to music, read some lyrics (in Ukrainian), and view photos of the singers.

Organizations and Embassies

▶ **Ukrainian Embassy**
3350 M Street NW
Washington, D.C. 20007
202-333-0606

▶ **Ukrainian Institute of Modern Art**
2318 West Chicago Avenue
Chicago, IL 60622
773-227-5522

▶ **Ukrainian Museum**
203 Second Avenue
New York, NY 10003

Index

Page numbers in *italics* indicate illustrations.

national parks and nature
   reserves, *34*
population, 83
resource, *76*
Tartar invasions, *46*
marmot, *28, 33*
Martos, Ivan, 111
Mazepa, Ivan, 49
miners in the Donets Basin, *78*
mining and energy, 78–80
missile plant, *74*
moloko (milk), 118
monesteries, 98–99
Mongols of the Golden Horde, 45, 48
Mongols on horseback, *45*
monuments
   kamianas babas (stone women),
      35, 35
   Motherland, 83
   Queen Olha, 43
mosques, 99
mountains, 23, 31–32
music, 9, 12, 108–110
musician, 8

N

national emblem, 15
national flag, *10, 10, 60,* 61
national parks, 33–36
natural resources, 53
   black soil (*chornozem*), 20, 22, 77
   mining and energy, 78–80
   natural gas, 19, 80
   petroleum, 80
nature reserves, 33–36
Nazi Germany, 54–55
Nitkitsky Botanical Garden, 36
Nobel Prize Winners, 86–87
North Atlantic Treaty Organization
   (NATO), 14
Northern Ukrainian Upland, 18–19

Novy Svet Nature Preserve, *33*
nuclear reactors, 80

O

oblasts (regions), 65
Odesa, 27, *27*
Oleh (Kyivan prince), 42
Olha (Kyivan queen), 43, *43*
Olympic Games, 115
opera houses, 109
Organization for Security and
   Cooperation in Europe, 68
Orthodox priest(s), *91, 93*

P

Paradzhanov, Serhiy, 107
Parliament and Ministry Building, 66
Partnership for Peace, 68
Paska (Easter bread), 95
people
   athletes, 112–115
   Cimmerians, 39–40
   daily life, 117–127
   education, 122–124
   emigration from Galicia, 51
   employment, 71, 73, 76, 81
   ethnic minorities, 84
   hospitality, 121–122
   immigration, 86
   marriage customs, 117
   miners, *78*, 78–79
   population, 83–84, 86
   Sarmatian horsemen, 40–41
   Scythian horsemen, 40
   Slavic, 41
   Trypillians, 39
   Ukrainian family, *116*
People's Front of Ukraine for
   Reconstruction (RUKH), 58

perestroika, 57
Peter the Great (Russia), 49
plant life
   forests, 29–30
   mountains, 31–32
   national parks, 33–36
   nature reserves, 33–36
   steppe, 32–33
Podkopayeva, Lilia, 115, *115*
Podlevsky, Volodymyr, 112
Polish-Lithuanian Commonwealth, 47
Polish rule, 46–49
Polissya Nature Reserve, 34
political parties, 66–67
population, 83–84
Potapenko, Vitaly (athlete), *114*
poultry vendors, *77*
presidency, 62–63
privatization, 71
Prokopov, Yevhen, 112
Prypyat Marshes, 20, 30
pysanky (Easter eggs), 102, *102*

R

rada (council), 48
radioactive contamination, 20, 21, 36
rally, *10*
rayons (counties), 65
religion, 12
   Byzantine Christianity, 43, 44
   Christianity, 91
   Constitutional freedom, 92
   denominations of Ukraine, 92
   Greek Catholic Church, 51, 55
   legalization, 57
   Orthodox calendar and holy days,
      94–96
   Paganism, 41, 44
   Roman Catholic, 47
   Russian Orthodox Church, 10, 53

Meet the Author

P
ATRICIA K. KUMMER writes and edits textbook materials and nonfiction books for children and young adults from her home office in Lisle, Illinois. She earned a Bachelor of Arts degree in history from the College of St. Catherine in St. Paul, Minnesota, and a Master of Arts degree in history from Marquette University in Milwaukee, Wisconsin. Before starting her career in publishing, she taught social studies at the junior high/middle-school level.

Since then, she has written about American, African, Asian, and European history for textbook publishers and "A Guide to Writing and Speaking" in World Book's *Word Power Library*. She wrote *Côte d'Ivoire* in the Children's Press series Enchantment of the World and thirty books about the states, including Washington, D.C., and Puerto Rico. *Côte d'Ivoire*, *Alabama*, *Hawaii*, and *New Mexico* won awards from Chicago Women in Publishing. The Illinois Press Women's Association gave awards to *Alabama*, *Hawaii*, *New Mexico*, *Tennessee*, *Washington, D.C.*, and *West Virginia*. One of her favorite projects was writing a commissioned biography for Jerry Reinsdorf, chairman of the Chicago Bulls and Chicago White Sox. The biography commemorates the life of his administrative assistant, who died leaving a three-year-old daughter. The book, based totally on interviews, will be presented to the daughter when she is about thirteen years old.

"Writing books about people, states, and countries requires a great deal of research," she says. "To me, that's the most fun part of a project. For this book, I started by sitting down at my computer and going online. I pulled up the latest information on Ukraine from the State Department, the CIA, and Encyclopedia Britannica. Then I compiled a list of the most recent books on Ukraine. From there I went to the library. For the books my library didn't have, I placed twenty-seven interlibrary loan requests. Of those requests, only two books never showed up. To keep up with political, economic, and sporting events in Ukraine, I checked the daily online press services.

"The best part of the research for this book was interviewing Ukrainian Americans who had recently visited Ukraine. They told me about special customs and foods and showed me examples of Ukrainian folk art. I also spent a day in Chicago's Ukrainian Village neighborhood, where I sampled bread and pastries in a Ukrainian bakery, picked up information from a Ukrainian travel agent, conducted research at the Ukrainian National Museum, and ate lunch of *borsch* and *varenyky* at Sak's Ukrainian Village Restaurant. In addition, I interviewed people in Ukraine and Ukrainian Americans in the United States and Canada via e-mail."

Photo Credits